The Cumberland Coast

Neil Curry

For Tony Raven
The Reader I Kept in Mind

BOOKCASE

Edmund Blood's "St. Michael" in Workington Parish Church

Contents

Preface
a very brief history of Cumberland

One Monday morning in 1974 the people of Cumberland woke up and found that their county no longer existed. As it so happened it was the morning of Monday 1st April, but this was no joke. They were now living in Cumbria. The government, with the assistance of an American management consultancy team, had amalgamated Cumberland with Westmorland, together with a piece of Yorkshire and parts of northern Lancashire to form this new county. Centuries of history had been overturned and by people living hundreds of miles away. It was a decision which was by no means universally popular.

Remote as Cumberland might seem to those living in the more populous south, the area has been settled for quite as long as any other part of the country, and some of its fifty or so stone circles may even pre-date Stonehenge. What the people were like who built them, or indeed why they built them will never be known. What is clear though is that to erect them would have required a good deal of practical engineering skill and some understanding of mathematics, so we should never underestimate the technical or intellectual abilities of these earlier Cumbrians.

We can also take it that they had a degree of organised industry, as there is evidence to show that the stone axes quarried up on Harrison Stickle in the Langdales were sent down to be polished in the sand dunes of Ravenglass, before, in some cases, being exported to distant parts of Europe. But after the demise of these people, of whom we know so tantalisingly little, the history of the area becomes even more opaque, until AD 79 and the arrival of the 20th Legion led by Agricola. From then on the Roman army of occupation governed the whole of northern England as far up as Hadrian's Wall, building forts and towns the likes of which the local inhabitants had never before beheld.

This military occupation lasted for four hundred years, a long time in the history of any area, so the sudden and total withdrawal of the legions in AD 410, to try to save Rome and the Empire itself, must have been a time of immense upheaval. If there hadn't been barbarism before the Romans arrived, there almost certainly would have been the moment they left. Imperialism would have given way to a dangerous power vacuum, which left local tribal chiefs and would-be warlords skirmishing among themselves for decades to come. Eventually, out of this chaos, emerged that rather shadowy thing, the Kingdom of Rheged, whose last king, Urien, was murdered in AD 590, whereupon it became part of the Scottish Kingdom of Strathclyde.

For hundreds of years it passed backwards and forwards between English and Scottish kings, sometimes the result of a battle, sometimes as a marriage settlement, sometimes no more than a political ploy.

One or two dates stand out. The Vikings sacked Carlisle in AD 842, and in AD 875 there is a reference to the *Kingdom of the Cumbri*. The last Celtic king, Dunmail, was defeated in AD 945 by Edmund, King of Northumbria, who gave Cumberland (and this is the first reference to it by this name) to Malcolm I of Scotland on the condition he would back him with military aid whenever called upon to do so. It is at this time that the title *Prince of Cumberland* is given to the heir to the Scottish throne, as Shakespeare clearly knew in *Macbeth*.

King Canute acquired it next, only to exchange it with the actual Macbeth for Lothian. Macbeth then granted it to Siward, Earl of Northumbria. At some stage it must then, rather dizzyingly, have been passed back to Strathclyde, as it was William Rufus who brought it under the control of the English Crown in 1092. But the Scots recaptured it during the reign of Stephen and it was left to Edward I, the Hammer of the Scots, to take it back in 1157, when it was described as 'the county of Carlisle', the designation County of Cumberland not appearing in the Sheriff's accounts until 1177. And so it was called until that fateful All Fools Day in 1974 when it became part of Cumbria.

The change, as I said, was not universally popular. The county names and that sense of identity that went with them were greatly missed at first and still are in some places. Certainly in the Furness Peninsular, where I live, there are people who regard themselves as Lancastrians to this day, and campaign for the restoration of the old boundaries. There is a society called *The Friends of Real Lancashire*.

But it was no kind of nostalgia which led me to keep the old county name in the title of this book. I was simply being practical. The Cumberland coast used to stretch from the Solway Firth to the Duddon Estuary and it remains an entity in itself. There is a *Cumbria Coastal Path* which follows that route, and then goes on as far as Silverdale, but the towns it passes through after Millom — Ulverston, Cartmel, Arnside — are not the same. They do not feel the same. The people are not the same. They may be Cumbrians, but they're not, and never were, part of Cumberland.

Cumbria today means Wordsworth and daffodils. It means the Old Man of Coniston, Windermere and Helvellyn. It means the gift shops in Ambleside, mint cake in Kendal and gingerbread in Grasmere. In short, it means the Lake District. But Millom is hardly thought of as being in the lake District and Whitehaven and Workington are quite definitely not. Countless books have been written about *The Lake District,* but the Cumberland Coast has largely been ignored. There are books about the history of its mines and about its ship-building, but what I have tried to give here is a picture of it as an entity in itself, yet with all its diversity: the industries which were once here, but also the miles of natural beauty which are still here, and the way that towns like Whitehaven are rediscovering themselves.

And the people. In the two years and more I have spent driving and walking up and down this coast there were so many I met and talked with and who, as soon as they found out what I was up to, wanted to talk to me — sometimes for hours on end. They were invaluable, and so if any of them happen to be reading this and remember meeting me, they should regard this book as being dedicated to them personally, with my heartfelt thanks.

One:

*The Solway. Tidal rivers and mud flats. Edward I
and the Border Wars. The Reivers. Hadrian's
Wall. Bowness-on-Solway. The Port Carlisle
Canal. The railways. The haaf-net fishermen.
Campfield Moss and the RSPB.*

Mud flats. If a poll were to be held to decide which were the most
unpromising landscapes on the whole of the planet, it is hard to imagine
what would come higher than mud flats, the exposed underbelly of the
sea. And yet in 1964 the Solway (whose very name comes from two Old
English words *sol* and *wæþ* meaning a muddy ford) was designated as an
Area of Outstanding Natural Beauty.

And it's true. It is. And one of the reasons why it is, I think, is that
it shares our restlessness. You could almost say it reflects our restlessness.
Where beauty is concerned we seem to favour most what lingers least:
rainbows and roses, sunsets, butterflies and the like. And an estuary is, of
its very nature, changing constantly. For one thing, there seems to be an

Monument to Edward I at Burgh by Sands

inordinate amount of sky towering above the Solway. To the east it may be a deep delphinium blue, with streaks of cirrus as thin as vapour trails, yet at the very same moment clouds the colour of a bad bruise can be bunching up over Criffel and patterning the sands with their shadows. And then there is low water followed by high water, followed by low water, followed by high water. And of course there are the sunsets.

Turner came here to paint them. And, in some of the last words Ruskin ever wrote, his thoughts went back to the shores of the Solway and the "…sands which the sunset gilded with its withdrawing glow."

At low water the River Eden is still there, constantly cutting its channel through a hundred and more square miles of sand and mud, while the tide may have withdrawn so far that there is no sign of salt water whatsoever. You could almost believe it was never coming back, and even when it does turn, it is all very surreptitious to start with, slowly sidling its way back up the gulleys and runnels. And it's then, when so little seems to be happening, that it is at its most dangerous. If you are too far out when those gulleys overflow, you can run for the shore, but there is a good chance the water will get there first. As an old local saying has it, "He who dreams on bed of Solway may wake up in the next world."

I remembered those words when I was dawdling through the Pre-Raphaelite room of the Walker Art Gallery in Liverpool recently. In a gloomy corner I had noticed one of those paintings of pale, wistful ladies with impossibly auburn, waist-length hair. Millais for sure. And it was. She was standing with her arms behind her back and it was some moments before I noticed that it was not a belt round her waist but a chain. The notes told me the picture was called *The Martyr of the Solway* and that she was Margaret Wilson of Wigton, a Covenanter who had stuck so firmly to her beliefs that on May 11th 1685 she had been chained to a stake in the Solway Firth and left to drown as the tide came in. I feel very sure that the real life Margaret Wilson would not have looked as demurely composed or as well-coiffeured as Millais shows her. What faith though and what a death. I found out later that this was the Scottish town of Wigton, not the Cumbrian one, but the horror of it is still the same.

Watching the tide coming in, I have often wondered just what weight and volume of water was on the move out there. In the summer, during a dry spell, when the rivers are beginning to run low, a really high tide may force the Eden back as far as Beaumont, and that's about four miles from Burghmarsh Point. But there must always come a time when it can go no further, a time when river and tide have to call a truce and for a brief moment or two there is a complete and total balance between them, with nothing moving at all. I saw it happen once. Out walking, I had decided to sit and have my lunch beside Rusland Pool, not far from where I live in Ulverston, and I suppose I was half aware that the river was going backwards, but I wasn't really taking much notice until I realised that it had stopped. It may have been the sudden silence that caught my attention. The water was dead still, an absolute calm for perhaps half a minute, and then slowly, very slowly the river re-asserted itself and began to push the tide back where it belonged. Shakespeare must have seen it somewhere too, perhaps while being rowed across the Thames to The Globe, for in Act III of *Anthony and Cleopatra* we read of a

> swan's down feather
> That stands upon the swell at the full of tide,
> And neither way inclines.

If you are watching from the shores of the estuary as the tide goes out, then at first the ever-widening expanse of wet sand and mud it leaves behind shows no signs of life at all: a landscape of surfaces, the shining levels, but underneath it is fidgeting with hidden creatures and after a short while you begin to notice a number of little damp coils and spirals, no more than an inch or so high. Worm casts. Soon there are more and more of them, but even so this is no indication of the enormous abundance of life that lies buried below. Shingle and rock can provide safe hiding places for crabs and snails, as well as hard surfaces for barnacles, limpets and such like to attach themselves to, but out there on the mud flats the only way for any creature to survive is to burrow, and if the dunlin, knot and oystercatchers that live off them are to be counted in their thousands then these crustaceans must surely number millions. Their empty shells decorate the shoreline: cockles, blue-black mussels, and those orange, pink and yellow tellins that look like little finger nails. And razor shells. Always empty. I have no idea what kind of slime-thing lives inside: straight, smooth and sharp, they can burrow down into the sand, so I've been told, faster than a spade can go after them.

10

Just as these vast spaces are a daily battle ground between the water and the land, so the flat countryside on either side of the Solway Firth was once a battleground for warring nations, and feuding clans for hundreds of years, and even the rivers themselves, the Eden and the Esk, being tidal and with scarcely more than a couple of miles between them in places, have from time to time played their own deadly part in the skirmishes. Cattle thieves, if they timed their raid properly, could have driven a stolen herd back through the rising waters and then had time to stand and gloat over their pursuers raging helplessly on the other side, powerless to get at them. On the other hand, if they'd bungled things, and were being chased and the tide was in, then they either stood their ground and fought it out, or took their chance in the waters. Two thousand Scots are said to have drowned in the Eden in 1216 doing just that after a raid on Holm Cultram Abbey.

Edward I, Edward Longshanks, knew all about these waters. Time and again he had led his armies north in those terrible wars of attrition he conducted. In 1295, when the Scots refused to pay their feudal levies and mustered an army at Selkirk, he advanced on Berwick, with 25,000 infantryman and a thousand cavalry. The military victory was a formality; what he intended was a demonstration of just what anyone who opposed him could expect. Over the course of three days, 11,000 men, women and children were massacred, and the city was burned to the ground. He understood how to inflict psychological blows too: taking Scotland's Stone of Destiny from the Abbey at Scone and having it installed at Westminster beneath the throne of England. He would reign supreme.

A ruthless and merciless man, he failed to see that actions of this kind do not quell an enemy, they incense them, and what followed were years of guerrilla warfare. But the *Hammer of the Scots* was not a man to change his tactics. When he finally overcame and captured Wallace he had him disembowelled, but then perhaps Edward had not forgotten that after the Battle of Stirling Bridge one of his own commanders had been flayed and his skin made into a belt for Wallace's broadsword. These were hard men living in hard times.

Even when he was approaching seventy, with his white hair flowing down over his shoulders, Edward still led his men personally, this time against Robert the Bruce. But by now time had caught up with him at last and in 1307 he died at Burgh-on-Sands, on the eve of a battle. Ever the strategist though, he had left orders for the flesh to be boiled off his bones so they could be carried against the Scots, but his son, Edward II had the body taken back to Westminster Abbey for burial, though it has been claimed that the entrails were interred in Holm Cultram Abbey.

There is a monument to him, erected in 1685 by the Duke of Norfolk, not far from Burgh, down a fly-infested lane, over a cow-cratered field and almost out on the marsh. Sir Walter Scott has Redgauntlet, the old Jacobite, celebrate it as a great landmark of Scottish liberty. "The just hand of Providence overtook him on that spot, as he was leading his bands to complete the subjugation of Scotland." It is hard to imagine anywhere more bleak, or any place worse to fight a battle, with the wind whipping in from the estuary and the ground so wet and so tussocky you'd be trying to keep one eye on your foe and one eye on the ground all the time, knowing that if you once fell you were finished.

The monument itself is a tall sandstone obelisk surmounted by a cross, and around it are those grisly railings you see in Victorian cemeteries – either to keep people out, or to keep the dear-departed in, I am never quite sure which. The plaque is impossible to read now as the bolts holding it in place have rusted and the stain run down obliterating the words. To complete the air of wretchedness, all the weeds inside the railed-off area were dead when I went there; some council workmen had clearly been round with the weed-killer and there was no sign of green, everything shrivelled and brown. It really was an *Ozymandias* moment: to think of Longshanks, who, like Shelley's antique king before him, might well have been minded to thunder, "Look on my works, ye Mighty and despair", commemorated by such a drab thing, and where the lone and level mud flats stretch far away.

So fought over was this whole area that life for the ordinary people who were trying to live there became quite insupportable. What was the point of raising cattle if they were always stolen? What was the point of growing crops if they were always trampled down or burned? The only sensible solution was to let someone else raise their cattle and then go and steal them, and steal their grain too, and whatever else you needed to live on. Those who had been robbed either went under or they robbed someone else in turn. The Old English verb for to rob and plunder was *reafian* and from it we get the word *reivers* — those "men who rode by moonlight", and who have become so romanticised, and again not least by Sir Walter Scott.

As the old rhyme has it;

The freebooter ventures both life and limb,
Good wife and bairn, and every other thing;
He must do so, or else must starve and die,
For all his livelihood comes of the enemnie.

Enemy here does not necessarily mean either Scottish or English; anyone not in your own clan or family might be, and often enough was your enemy, hence the long-lasting blood feuds between the Maxwells and the Johnstones, the Scotts and the Elliotts, and between the Armstrongs and practically everybody. It is true that the reivers' work — and they do seem to have regarded it as work — involved great danger, necessitated great bravery and was likely to end in a violent death, either by the sword or the gallows. But romantic? Hecky Noble can hardly have thought it romantic when Dickie Armstrong of Dryhope attacked him with a hundred of his clansmen, stole two hundred head of cattle, destroyed nine houses and ended by burning his son alive, together with his daughter-in-law who was pregnant at the time. In his book on the Border Reivers, *The Steel Bonnets*, George MacDonald Fraser puts it succinctly. It was a time, he says, "when the great Border tribes, both English and Scottish, feuded continuously among themselves, when robbery and blackmail were everyday professions, when raiding, arson, kidnapping, murder and extortion were an important part of the social system."

One way to protect yourself if you were outside the powerful feuding families was to pay for such protection, and the word for it, the word the Reivers added to our language, was *blackmail*. So-called, according to one explanation because it was a *black* or illegal rent. Another suggestion is that if people were too poor to pay in cash then they were obliged to pay in meal or corn. "Soe that this briberye they call Blackmeale, in respect that the cause for which yt is taken is foule and dishonest."

One curious way of trying to put an end to this abuse was a Scottish Act of Parliament of 1567 which made the *paying* of blackmail an offence punishable by death. Why does such a stupid decision by a government not surprise me? The poor were suddenly in a no-win situation and it was another twenty years before proceedings were taken against those demanding the blackmail.

The rich and the powerful, who were by no means less vulnerable to assault, protected themselves inside those Pele Towers which are still such a feature of the Border landscape. The towers did not need to be large; they were intended as places of refuge against sudden attack and not meant to hold out against a siege. Stone-built, with walls which might be up to ten feet thick, they could not be burned down and the only entrance was through a heavy, narrow door reinforced with iron. If raiders did manage to get inside, then the only staircase was a spiral one which turned anti-clockwise so that a defender would have his sword arm free, unlike his attacker.

To build such a tower of course required money and in areas where no one family could afford this, then a combined effort was sometimes made to fortify the church tower and at least two examples can still be seen in the Solway area: at Burgh (a name which means *stronghold)* and at Newton Arlosh.

Violence was endemic in the whole area, but never more so than in a stretch of land between the Esk and the Sark measuring little more than 12 miles by 5. This was a lawless buffer zone where the situation was so out of control that neither side wanted to accept responsibility for it, yet neither was ready to admit that the other owned it. Fittingly, it went by the name of *The Debateable Land.* The two governments hit on a scheme which they seem to have thought would put an end to all the troubles. They issued a declaration which read, "That all Scotsmen and Englishmen from this time forth shall be free to rob, burn, spoil and slay any person or animals or goods belonging to all who inhabit The Debateable Lands." The result, which, curiously, they do not seem to have anticipated, was a bloody free-for-all that lasted until the Act of Settlement in 1552 when an agreed border was established which ran, not along the Esk, as it so often had, but along the Sark.

On the ground, in real terms, the Settlement was little more than a diplomatic nicety, as the border had been there, or thereabouts, for some fourteen hundred years, since Roman times. There must, I imagine, have been a time when the very notion of a boundary to the Roman Empire would have seemed almost treasonable. A wall could look like an admission of defeat, an acceptance of the fact that they were not going any further. Their aim had been to conquer and occupy the entire known world. But by the first century AD that was no longer looking to be a wise idea and it was decided to call a halt to any further expansion. Other frontiers of the Empire were often clearly demarcated by some natural boundary, such as a river, an ocean, or, as in North Africa, a desert, but when the Emperor Hadrian came to Britain to assess the situation, he does not seem to have liked what he found. He withdrew the legions from the Forth-Clyde isthmus, brought them down to the Tyne-Solway gap and began the construction of a defensive wall, which was to run 84 miles from Newcastle to Bowness-on-Solway.

Today it is a World Heritage Site, but at the same time it has been established as a recognised coast to coast walk, which is attracting countless thousands of visitors whose boots are beginning to erode what it was hoped would be protected. Depending on which direction people decide to go, Bowness-on-Solway is either the start or the finish of their walk and down on the shoreline on a little Edwardian promenade, known as The Banks, there is a tiny pavilion, which, in both Latin and English, either welcomes them, or cheers them off on the first leg of the way. *Fortuna vobis adsit. Good Luck Go With You.* There is also an ink pad and a little rubber stamp, as a full "passport" of such stamps entitles the walker to purchase "an exclusive souvenir badge and certificate". What is conspicuously not there, however, is any trace of the wall itself, unless, that is, you look closely at some of the older houses in the village and at the west wall of the church, where there is some very well-dressed stone.

Bowness-on-Solway could not be more different from Bowness-on-Windermere. No Vinegar Joe's. No gift shops, or outdoor clothing shops. In fact no shops at all. Everywhere is peace and quiet, but it can't always have been so, and certainly not in the days of the Wall. It does take a massive leap of the imagination now to envisage Roman soldiers walking about here. Yet for some three hundred years there were – eight hundred to a thousand of them. Maia, (meaning *The Greater*) the name of the fort they were based in, was the second largest along the entire Wall complex, and covered an area of over seven acres. Where today the well-tended gardens are, there would have been barrack blocks and officers' quarters, storehouses and stables, workshops, cookhouse and mess halls. And there were not only soldiers. Outside the south gate are traces of a *vicus*, a civilian settlement, where the hangers-on lived, running the shops, no doubt an inn, and probably a brothel. Everywhere there would have been noise and activity: training exercises, manoeuvres, and shouted commands from the parade ground. Walking through the village after a meal in the King's Arms, thought to be located at the very centre of the camp, I passed one other person – a man out with his dog. We nodded to each other and said Good Evening.

Even St Michael's Church has not always been so peaceful. In 1626 a raiding party from over the water in Scotland somehow managed to steal the church bells, and make off with them, but they didn't get far. The aggrieved parishioners were soon after them, and with the raiders' boat so heavily weighed down, their only way of escape was to dump the bells overboard into the Solway, at a place now known as *Bell Dub*. The Bowness men were not going to leave it at that though and before long they made a return trip, stealing the bells from *two* villages: Dornock and Middlebrie. And they are still there today in the church, but since new ones were bought in 1905, they no longer ring out but are to be seen standing on the floor behind the font. It is a tradition apparently for each new priest appointed to Annan to write to the vicar of St Michael's and ask for their return, and the reply, traditionally, is always the same: *Yes, certainly, when we can have ours back.* A long-standing joke apparently. Oddly though, the bells were loaned to Annan in 1955 for the opening of their museum, but only for a fortnight; then they came back to Bowness. There are traditionalists on both sides, it would seem.

In the nineteenth century attempts were being made to bring this quiet part of the country into line with the great industrial developments of the age. Carlisle was thriving, but it needed access to the sea. The River Eden certainly ran down to the sea, but with all its twists and turns and the tides in the Solway Firth, it had never been commercially feasible. A canal looked to be the answer and in 1819 the navigators were brought north and they began digging. It took them four years to dig their way the eleven miles to a little village just east of Bowness called Fisher's Cross, which, when the canal was opened in March 1823, was given the grander and incorrigibly optimistic name of Port Carlisle. It had cost £90,000 and needed eight locks to negotiate the drop of sixty feet, but vessels could now be towed into the centre of the city in just under two hours, and it was possible to travel by water from Carlisle to Liverpool in a single day. People must have marvelled at the speed of change. Now it is all history. Hesket House, on the edge of Port Carlisle, which has a fragment of a Roman altar stone embedded above its lintel, was once a hotel – the Steam Packet Inn it was called and it was where emigrants stayed while waiting for a passage, via Whitehaven and Liverpool, to Ellis Island and their new life in the United States. What tension, fear and excitement it must have known in its time. What tears too.

But it was a gala day in Carlisle when the canal was opened. As the first vessel, the *Robert Burns*, reached the Canal Basin the band played *Hearts of Oak* and *Rule Britannia*, flags were flying and cannons fired a Royal Salute. The workers were given free bread and cheese and when all the speeches and public formalities were over then the festivities began for the dignitaries. According to one report, "At 4pm, the committee, carrying white sticks to distinguish them from the rest of the vast crowd, marched behind a band via Caldewgate and English Street back to the Bush Inn, and with 150 shareholders sat down to an elegant and sumptuous dinner. No less than 33 toasts were drunk and it went on for 12 hours, finishing with a lavish ball at the Crown and Mitre Hotel." The town must have been very quiet the next day.

Sad to say, the canal was never the success its founders had hoped it would be, or as the celebrations would seem to have promised. Perhaps its greatest moment of glory was in 1829 when Stephenson's *Rocket* was shipped along it on its way to the Liverpool-Manchester railway. But it was the development of the railway which brought about its closure, with the opening of the Carlisle to Lancaster line proving to be just too much competition. By 1854 the canal had been drained and a railway track, the final insult, laid along its bed. That too eventually closed, but not until 1932.

Another, and truly enterprising railway scheme was the opening of the line between Bowness and Annan. To avoid a detour through Carlisle, the Solway Junction Railway Co. built a viaduct over the estuary. One mile and 176 yards long, built of iron, and with 193 piers, it was a spectacular piece of engineering.. It opened for goods traffic in 1869 and began carrying passengers over its scenic route in 1870. But it was not long before it too was having its troubles. The winter of 1880/81 was so severe that the Esk and the Eden both froze solid and when the thaw came and the ice melted, there were what amounted to small icebergs – measuring up to thirty square yards and ten feet thick ramming into it at some fifteen miles an hour. Forty-five of the piers collapsed, leaving a gap which took three years to repair. It continued to be in general use up to the beginning of the First World War, but was then restricted to light goods traffic and finally closed in 1921. But only closed to rail traffic, it would seem, as it is said that Scotsmen in need of a drink on a Sunday night, when their own pubs were shut, would walk across it into England, but that not all of them were steady enough to manage the walk back, which may be one reason why it was totally demolished in 1935.

I had been told I might meet up with the haaf netters near the old railway embankment as they came back on shore when the tide turned. I was there shortly before nine o'clock. The tide was still out, but there was no one to be seen. I was disappointed, but it didn't matter too much – the air was fresh and the sunlight still had some of that early morning brightness to it. I walked along the shore for a while, crunching shells, and heading back in the direction of the village, when a redshank's warning call — strident and sudden — came from somewhere out over the sands and I tried to find it through my binoculars, but couldn't. Instead, what I did see were two tiny figures way out in the middle of the channel – haaf fishers. If sunlight had not flickered on the bright yellow waterproofs they were wearing I might never have noticed them. They were standing chest deep in the flow. Once I knew what to look for I found half a dozen others, dark blobs only for the most part.

The name for the net they use, the *haaf,* comes from an Old Norse word meaning a *channel* and this type of fishing in the Solway channel probably dates back more than a thousand years. A *haaf net* is not something you can go into a shop and buy like a fishing rod. Each one has been made by hand, and they are big. The net itself is suspended from a 16 foot horizontal beam supported on three 5 foot legs. Sixteen feet also happens to be the length of a Viking oar and it is thought that the original *haaf* beams had in fact been *re-cycled*, as it were. Once out in the channel, the fishermen place this framework across the flow of the current, then standing behind it and holding on to the central upright, allow the net to billow out behind them, keeping a strand or two wrapped around their fingers so as to feel immediately if a fish should swim in. Then all you do is wait. Nothing to it – except for the fact that the net can weigh up to fifty pounds when dry, and you are constantly having to shift your feet on the slippery mud to make sure you don't get mired in and start to sink, and at the same time fighting to keep your balance against the weight of an eight knot tide pushing against you. And without an experienced and a knowing eye that can read those waters, and strong, quick wrists that can give a flick to the net when a fish does get into it, all you are going to get out there is very cold and wet. How the early Vikings ever survived, working in seawater up to their chests in the "waterproofs" they must have had we will never know.

When the tide turned and the two fishermen I had first spotted, Walter Graham and Frank Gate, came walking ashore it looked as though each of them was carrying a small set of football goal posts, but the canvas bags they had hanging down behind their backs were empty. They had stood in the water for two hours and caught nothing. A tough way of life it must always have been, but it is no longer a way of life on the Solway. There are no professional fishermen any more. For Water and Frank and their colleagues it is, as they say, a "pastime".

It is not, however, a pastime they are being allowed to enjoy in peace. The Environmental Agency, which charges them £100 for a licence to fish, has decided that they are responsible for the decline in the salmon stocks, and so have cut their season by half. Whereas they were once allowed to fish from 1st March until 9th September, since 2000 they can not begin fishing until 1st June. Oddly enough, on the private estates upriver, the wealthy rod fishermen, with the big businesses and the corporate entertainment people behind them, were given an exemption and they can fish from 15th January until 14th October. The ban was aimed solely at the working-class men from Carlisle and the Solway villages. They fought the decision and eventually raised enough money to appeal to the High Court, but the judge ruled that Fisheries Minister, Elliot Morley, was within his rights to do what he had. Rights.

It does look as though salmon fishing in the Solway area has always been contentious. Thinking back to Scott's *Redgauntlet* I remember that it was the attack on the Quakers' stake-nets that was the beginning of the troubles. "I tell you in fair terms, Joshua Geddes, that you and your partners are using unlawful craft to destroy the fish in the Solway by stake-nets and weirs; and that we, who fish fairly, and like men, as our fathers did, have daily and yearly less sport and less profit."

No, the situation is not new and neither are the arguments. In an article in *The Scots Magazine* of February 1967 we read that, "…in view of the terms of the Hunter Report, which aims ultimately at the curtailment of all forms of net fishing for salmon, the future of the haaf-netter is not too promising — a prospect, it may be added, which causes no despondency among the rod and line men." The Hunter Report had advocated "commercial and research schemes" (fish farms) and hoped they would be started quickly, "so that fishing for sea salmon may be discontinued soon." That the pollution coming from fish farms may be one of the causes of the decline in the numbers of wild salmon is not something that comes up so readily for official discussion.

And the situation has not improved any. In August 2004 the Environment Agency sent down a group of water bailiffs to conduct a two month covert investigation codenamed (have they no sense of shame?) *Viking*. Walter said it was not very "covert" as they could see them hiding behind the gorse bushes. As a result though, nineteen local men were arrested and charged with falsifying their catch records.

For reasons one can only guess at, there seems to be a wish among certain people to put an end to a thousand years of haaf net fishing. "We are a dying breed," said Walter. I hope he is wrong.

But a mile or so south, down along the coast road, in the RSPB Reserve of Campfield Moss, everything seems to be breeding and flourishing. It was early July when I went there first, one of the quietest times of year for birds. The geese – the Barnacle and the Pink Foot – for which the Solway Firth is famous, were all still away on their breeding grounds in Greenland, Iceland or Svalbard, but come September and October and the darker days of winter, there would be 30,000 of them there, I was told, as well as perhaps 9,000 knot and 6,000 dunlin, all feeding off the snails, the worms and the shrimps. It's then that the figures, like stars and galaxies, begin to run out of control. The Baltic tellin alone, it seems, can number more than four thousand to the cubic yard.

But if there are no barnacles on the mud flats and the salt marshes, what brings the Barnacle geese? John Gerard, writing in 1597 in his

The stolen bells at St. Michael's, Bowness on Solway

Herball offered an explanation. "There are found in the North parts of Scotland and the Islands adjacent, called Orchades," he wrote, "certaine trees whereon do grow certaine shells of a white colour… wherein are contained little living creatures: which shells in time of maturity doe open and out of them grow those little living things, which falling in to the water do become fowles, which we call Barnacles." He is adamant about it. "What our eies have seen, and our hands have touched we shall declare." There is even a drawing to illustrate the sequence of events.

If this all seems a but dubious, then the age that Barnacle geese can live to is as surprising, but well authenticated in a diary kept John Ostle, who lived at The Nook, near Newtown, two or three miles south of Silloth in the middle of the nineteenth century. He tells us he caught one on the shore in 1843. "It is the best weather-glass — it shouts before a storm — and is a splendid ornament, a proper sight to behold." And he records its death in 1874. "The Barnacle goose died. It had been with me for 31 years." The life expectancy of the working man was not much more in those days. and recording its 27th birthday in February 1870 he observed that, "It looks no older now than when I caught it." Which is an odd an

Haaf-net fishermen

enviable thing about birds. They do never seem to age. Whoever could harness their secret is made for life, as it were.

I had meant to ask Dave Blackledge, the RSPB warden who took me on a tour of the reserve what he thought of Gerard's theory, but I forgot..

The life of an RSPB warden sounds idyllic – wandering around in your wellies, with your binoculars round your neck and looking at the birds, but the truth is that for most of the time it is land management and sheer hard graft. And in all weathers.

It was in the late 80's that the RSPB bought North Plain Farm. The families who had worked the land in this area for generations had of course drained it for crops and pasturage, but the RSPB's plan was to reverse all this and restore the natural wet conditions which had prevailed long before the advent of farming. As a result there are now redshanks, curlews, oystercatchers and lapwings nesting there again, birds with some of the most distinctive and evocative cries one can ever hear. At a distance, a lapwing seems to be just a black and white bird, but close to it becomes almost exotic. We see their raised crests, and the orange rump, and what had looked to be black is now an iridescent green with touches of purple and copper. Definitely one of my favourite birds. One of Dave's too, he said. And the numbers are rising. They now have thirty nesting pairs on the farmland and out on the mosses, which is good news, as, near where I live, I remember there being almost that many in a wet field where the footbridge crosses the Crake at Greenodd. And now there are none.

Farmland birds have also been in decline recently and so as well as restoring the wetlands, they have planted barley and quinoa in an attempt to bring them back and the results have been spectacular. In September 2000 when flocks began to gather they counted 400 linnets and over a thousand skylarks. Truly and exaltation of larks. The hedgerows are being managed too – cut and layered by hand instead of being decapitated by a machine and one very cunning way of getting it done, and getting it done really well, was by holding a hedge-laying competition on their land. Some good thinking there.

Beyond the fields there is an area of what is known as lowland raised peat bog, which has its own particular insect and plant life. Thanks to garden centres, where peat is sold by the sackload, this is fast becoming

Dave Blackledge, RSPB Warden

one of the rarest wildlife habitats in the country, but English Nature together with the RSPB have managed to conserve it by damming up the old drains, cutting out the invading birch and so raising the water level and encouraging the growth of the moss. It is the various sphagnum mosses which are the key to the development of a raised bog. Rootless, they absorb moisture through their leaves and form a thick living skin just above the water table. Walking across it you never feel altogether safe though; it feels as if it could swallow you. Few other plants seem able to survive in the water-logged, airless and acidic conditions which develop and the dead sphagnum sinks down to form the peat, to a depth sometimes of up to fifty feet.

Cotton grass and bog myrtle are two exceptions which do manage to thrive there and this is now one of the few places where bog myrtle can still be found. The cotton grass waves its little handkerchiefs in the wind

The Solway Firth

and if you crush the leaves of the bog myrtle between your fingers the eucalyptus-like smell it gives off is said to be an excellent insect repellent – especially against fleas!

Although lapwings were the only birds we saw on the mosses that day, Dave took me to where he had laid out some short lengths of corrugated iron to encourage the sort of reptile that likes the damp and the dark, but being cold-blooded will also enjoy the extra warmth it gives when the metal heats up. The first he lifted had a lizard under it. I couldn't remember the last time I had seen a lizard in this country. Under the next there was a young toad, squat and crouched like a little Sumo wrestler. And alongside the third, just as he was about to lift it, he pointed out an adder, curled up there, its colour and the zigzag markings down its back making it an almost exact match with the dead bracken around it. It didn't move, which was not surprising: it's the bright day that brings forth the adder, and being solar-powered in our climate does have its drawbacks. And we ourselves only just made it, running back to Dave's caravan, before the rain came down – sheets of it and cold too. "Rain, rain, rain. The young swallows that came out are shivering and ready to starve." That was Gilbert White writing in his diary on 8th July, the same day, in 1777. It might not have been quite as bad as that, but it was wet, and it was cold. Well, after all, this was Cumberland.

Two:

Holm Cultram Abbey – fires and restorations.
Michael Scot. Matthew Deveys. Skinburness.
Moricambe Bay. Newton Arlosh. Sarah Losh and
Wreay. Two serial murderers. Silloth: the railway;
the dock; the bathing resort. Kathleen Ferrier.
Carr's Flour Mill. Shrimps.

To get to Silloth, if you are coming from the north, you can either keep close to the coast and wind your way through Newton Arlosh, or stay on the straighter roads and pay your respects to Melvyn Bragg's Wigton. Whichever way, you have to pass through Abbeytown, which can't really claim to be much of a town and does not even have an abbey

Above: Holm Cultram Abbey

26

any more. On the Ordnance Survey map it says only, *Abbey* (rems of), yet Holm Cultram Abbey, to give it its full and proper name, once ranked in importance alongside Fountains and Riveaulx. And what is just as curious is that, despite what the map says, there are no remains, at least none to be seen above ground, no trace at all of the cloisters, dormitory, refectory, chapter house and so on which must once have been there. The hulking parish church, which claims to *be* the abbey, puts me in mind of Washington's axe, which is said to have had its head replaced a couple of times and the handle too.

It is such an ugly building, grim, muscle-bound, and totally out of proportion with itself, even the headstones in the churchyard are massive, and it is set in what are now the most unlikely of surroundings: an assortment of pebble-dashed council houses, and retirement bungalows festooned with hanging-baskets. It looks almost embarrassed to find itself there.

{And though it would be hypocritical of me to take back a word of what is written here, I have to say that I was saddened a year after I had written it to learn that the place had been gutted by fire, and no accidental fire either, but mindless, wilful arson. The fire was started in the vestry where the flames spread up the panelling and in no time the whole place was alight. The fire brigade managed to save the basic structure of the building, but the roof burnt through and fell in. When I went to see it a week later, the smell of smoke was bad enough in itself, but then it began to rain. The mess inside the church was beyond belief. There are plans to rebuild it, even though the cost is going to be between two and three million pounds.}

If there is no trace of the actual Abbey, you don't have to go far to realise what happened to it; the red sandstone farms buildings in the surrounding area would be enough in themselves, but, if any further proof were needed, then at Abbey House Farm, set into the walls of one of the cow-sheds, there is the gargoyle of a monk, mouth wide open, shouting, yawning or maybe gurning. Applegarth Farm nearby, which must have been where the Abbey's orchards once were, has some distinguished armorials set into the walls of its milking parlour, and at Raby Cote one of the barns bears the carved rebus of Robert Chambers, the Abbot who built the splendid porch over the church's west doorway early in the sixteenth century.

The Abbey was founded in 1150 by a group of monks from Melrose in Scotland. The whole of Cumberland was under Scottish rule at that time, having been ceded by the usurper Stephen in 1136, and Prince of Cumberland was then the title Scottish monarchs conferred on their chosen heir. Henry, Prince of Cumberland, it was, the eldest son of King David of Scotland, who gave the monks their land and granted them their charter. On the face of it, it would look to have been a generous act, but perhaps not all *that* generous, as the land was waste, a conglomeration of moorland, marsh and untouched forest. The name tells us as much, *holm* being an Old Norse word for a piece of raised ground among wet marshland. The meaning of *Cultram* is less clear and so has invited a good deal of speculation, some of it rather imaginative, like the suggestion that it is an abbreviation of the Latin *culturam terram,* cultivated land, but as it bore the name long before the land *was* cultivated, that clearly will not do. Things are not helped any by an Appendix to a study of the Abbey by G.E. Gilbanks which lists more than fifty variant spellings of the name. In all likelihood, at some time in its past it was a *ham,* or homestead, belonging to a Saxon whose name must at least have begun with a C. Beyond that, all is guesswork; which of course does not stop people guessing.

But *Culturam terram* it did become before very long. The monks were Cistercians, an austere offshoot of the Benedictine Order, and they were not simply contemplatives; they believed that *To Work is to Pray.* From sandstone quarried in Scotland, shipped across the Solway and up the River Waver, they built a cruciform church which was at every point larger than the Priory at Carlisle. With nine bays, it was 279 feet long and 135 feet wide with a tower that reached 114 feet — 4 feet higher than Carlisle. (It almost looks deliberate) And an old tradition has it that seven priests could offer mass without interrupting each other, which suggests at least six side chapels.

Devout as the Cistercians certainly were, they were also very astute when it came to business and money. They cleared the forests, drained the marshes and by Edward I's time, the early 1300's, they were exporting thirty *sacks* of wool a year, and as a sack contained two hundred fleeces, we can see that they were grazing at least 6000 sheep. Within twenty five years of the Abbey's foundation they had established five working farms, providing enough grain to require the building of outlying granaries such as that at Silloth.

Over the years the monks acquired more and more land, stretching as far south as Workington. Inevitably wealth on such a scale began to call attention to itself. In 1216 Alexander II of Scotland invaded Cumberland to avenge the attack King John had made on Berwick. His troops sacked Carlisle and then, ignoring his orders to leave the religious houses alone, they plundered Holm Cultram, making off with horses, cattle, books, vestments, and the holy vessels from the altar. It is even said that they stripped the covers from a monk who lay dying in the infirmary. But sacrilege of this nature could hardly be expected to go unpunished. It was February; the days were short, and when they tried to get back across the Eden there was an exceptionally high tide coupled with a strong west wind. Two thousand of them are said to have drowned. "A revenge worthy of an offended God," as the Chronicler put it. After the death of Edward I the Scottish raids became so frequent that the monks had to petition the king for aid as "they were so impoverished that they could not serve God without help." In 1322 Robert the Bruce attacked and desecrated the place even though his own father was buried there! It was about this time that the monks built a castle at Wolsty to safeguard what treasures they had left, and before the century was out there is a record of them paying £200 to the Earl of Douglas to ransom the church and lands, which sounds very much like protection money in the age-old Reiver tradition. But the time would come when the abbey attracted attention of a very different kind — from Henry VIII and there was nothing to protect it then. Abbot Thomas Carter did join the opposition group known as The Pilgrimage of Grace and was probably involved in the attack on Carlisle and while it is not known for certain, it seems more than likely that he was hanged along with the Abbots of Fountains, Riveaulx and Melrose. Henry took his religion very seriously.

It has to be said that before the dissolution of the monasteries some of them were rather dissolute. Thomas Carter himself was accused of "bringing women in to dine". But the story of Abbot Deveys might have been scripted by Umberto Ecco. When Matthew Deveys was elected in 1531 his appointment failed to meet with the approval of a monk by the name of Gawyn Borrodaile. In fact we are told that Borrodaile had "a great disdain" for him and it was not long before Deveys was found dead, clearly from a dose of poisoning. Borrodaile was accused and sent to Furness Abbey, where he was kept under what amounted to house arrest for almost six months. There was an 'examination' at which one witness said he heard Borrodaile claim that "Rather than Matthew Deveys were Abbot he would kill him with his own hands." Another reported seeing him standing next to the cook the night Deveys died. But Borrodaile must have had some influential friends as he does not seem to have been punished in any way and was in fact appointed as Abbot shortly before Thomas Cromwell finally decided in 1538 that Holm Cultram should be surrendered to the Crown.

The local people petitioned to be allowed to keep the church and it was agreed. It was also agreed, perhaps to no one's great surprise, that Gawyn Borrodaile should stay on as rector, a post he retained until his death in 1552. He was clearly a survivor.

It is nice to see family loyalty so strong that one of his descendents, Thomas Salkeld Borrodaile, set up a memorial plaque to him in 1900, just to the right of the organ. He calls him "A Good Borderer". I am not sure what that means, nor am I sure of the propriety of claiming to be descended from a monk, but that's families for you.

The rest of the Abbey fell into disrepair, especially as people began to take away the lead and the stone to meet their own building needs, and on 1st January 1600 the tower fell down, nearly killing the Vicar and one of his parishioners. After a few years it was decided to do some repairs and it is then that farce creeps in. On 18th April, 1604, "one Christopher Hardon, carrying a live coal and a candle into the roof of the church to search for an iron chizil which his brother had left there, and the wind being exceeding strong and boisterous it chanced that the coal blew out of his hand into a daw's nest, which was within the roof of the church and forthwith kindled the same, which set the roof on fire in such a great sort that within less than three hours it consumed and burnt both the body of the chancil and the whole church except to the south side of the low church which was saved by means of a stone vault."

The fire record of Cumberland churches is quite astonishing.

Since then, every hundred years or so, it has been subjected to prolonged bouts of restoration and rebuilding, the last as recently as the 1960's, and each no doubt directed by people who thought that they knew best. Now, as a result, there are six bays where once there were nine, no tower where once there was a tower, a new concrete floor, and, before the latest fire, a new oak roof and new oak pews. Yet there is a board outside which claims this is Holm Cultram. Clearly it is not. It is clearly a case of Washington's axe.

After so many years, and all it has gone through, it has deserved better than this; {it certainly never deserved another fire} better than being left stranded here, attached to a Gift Shop which opens only in the late afternoon and early evening when there is no one about. Perhaps what it really deserves is a return visit from Michael Scot. And who is Michael Scot? The name is so ordinary, so absolutely innocuous, that he might well be the borough surveyor, or a man from English Heritage, whereas in fact, in his own day, Michael Scot was regarded as a necromancer and a wizard of such high renown that he was written about by both Dante and Boccaccio, and for a while he lived here in Holm Cultram, when it *was* Holm Cultram. He was that *Wizard of the North* whom Walter Scott described in *The Lay of the Last Minstrel* as:

> A wizard of such dreadful fame
> That when in Salamanca's cave
> Him listed his magic wand to wave
> The bells would ring in Notre Dame.

Quite an achievement and the power did not pass away with him. After his death his books were said to have been kept in Holm Cultram's stronghold at Wolsty Castle, but were regarded as being so dangerous that no one dared open, let alone read them and so they moulded slowly away to dust.

Yet there was a totally different side to, or certainly a totally different view of Michael Scot. In the early years of the thirteenth century he was regarded as one of the foremost intellects in Europe and many of the books he wrote are still to be found stored away in some of Europe's ancient libraries and in the Vatican and the Bodleian. He had been born about 1180, somewhere in the Lowlands of Scotland, and after taking minor orders he studied at the universities of Oxford, Paris, Bologna, and Cordova, acquiring such a reputation for his learning in mathematics, law,

31

science and theology that he was appointed as tutor to Frederick II, King of Sicily, and then moving on, when his young pupil no longer need him, to Toledo. At that time Toledo was one of the great intellectual centres of Moorish Spain and there he joined a group of scholars and translators who were engaged in some of the most important literary enterprises of the age. Michael Scot it was who translated Aristotle from Arabic into Latin. A brilliant mathematician, he was also an alchemist at a time when alchemists were not dismissed as dreamers and fools but were making genuine advances in chemistry, metallurgy and pharmacy. He was equally renowned as an astronomer and when he returned to Frederick's Court he was appointed to the position of Royal Astrologer – astrology being regarded then as the more practical side of astronomy. It was all this intellectual achievement which probably lay behind his later reputation as a wizard. Anyone looking into his personal library and notebooks, particularly after his return to the rather less cultured North of his birth, and seeing there pages of Arabic, together with the different kinds of notation systems employed in algebra and astrology, would not have taken long to come to the wrong conclusion. And as his patron, Frederick, although a man of great erudition himself and a supporter of the arts, had been excommunicated more than once for opposition to the Pope, he was not without enemies eager to blacken his name and damn him as a heretic.

He had also become, one might say, a personality, and so legends sprang up about him, some fearsome, some rather light-hearted. In one of the latter a witch used his own stick to turn him into a hare and he was pursued by his own pack of hounds. By way of revenge, once he had extricated himself from that dilemma, he placed a charm in the eaves of her house so that as soon as she went through the door she started to dance and could not stop. And anyone else who went in to see what was happening started dancing too. He did relent, but not until they were all ready to drop, if they had been able. On another occasion he encountered a coven of witches celebrating their Sabbat and promptly turned them into stone. And they are still standing there to this day at Little Selkeld: Long Meg and her Daughters.

It was said he had the power to summon demons and the gift of prophecy. It was even claimed he had predicted his own death: saying that he would be killed by a stone falling on his head. And that came true:

a stone, loosened by the pulling of a bell rope, or so we are told, did fall on him and kill him while he was celebrating mass. Knowing what we do of the stonework at Holm Cultram, this is by no means impossible. Holm Cultram long insisted that he was buried there, but Melrose and Burgh-by-Sands made the same claim, and we will never know, as we will never know what the real truth is about Michael Scot.

A commonplace-sounding name it might be, but the area does have some decidedly uncommon ones too. Blitterlees is one and driving from Abbeytown to Silloth you pass a farm which proudly and clearly displays its name: Longcummercaitiff. I could look it up in Sedgefield's *Place Names of Cumberland and Westmorland*, but I would rather not, as I might find out it was perfectly explicable and that would spoil it. Seeing it made me remember another unusual name on the World War Two honours board in the Abbey: John Wm. Longcake of the Border Regiment. Apparently the family have lived in the area for over five hundred years and Longcake's ice-cream was once world famous in Silloth.

Then comes the sign for Skinburness, which does not, as I have seen it suggested, mean *Demon-haunted stronghold.* It is nothing quite so romantic. It is made up of three Old Norse elements and is the headland (*ness*) on which there was a shining (*skina*) fort (*burgh*). We know that the Romans built a series of mileforts from Bowness down to Maryport to defend the coastline south of the wall, and the end of this promontory would have been an obvious site for a fort, and also for some kind of beacon to warn vessels in danger of running aground on it, or to guide them into the safe waters of Moricambe Bay. The very end of the promontory is known as Grune Point and Grune being the Old Norse for *snout,* it is clear that this was very much a Viking area and that they too had possibly set up some kind of beacon here.

Perhaps we should call them Norsemen rather than use that emotive word Vikings, as those whose landed here do not seem to have arrived as raiding parties in the dreaded dragon-ships. The existence of both English and Norse place names among the villages shows that they did not come with the intention of wiping out the local population. They integrated. They were settlers, indeed they might even have been fugitives themselves, driven out of Ireland and not given to violence at all. It would have been a good place to settle – fertile land and seas rich in fish. And it is still a good place to be; the walk from Skinburness to Grune Point is a delight, especially in June and July when the thrift is in flower and the black-headed gulls still have their summer faces on, like maskers in some Venetian Carnival. Often you can have the whole place to yourself, the saltmarsh stretching away under a generous sky, curlews and oyster-catchers calling, and so much to find along the beach: cuttlebones, mermaids' purses, starfish, sea urchins, hundreds of little white empty crabs, and sometimes, not so pleasant, a rash of glinting jellyfish as big as hub caps.

At the end of Grune Point, and almost overgrown now, there is a reminder of another time when coastal defence was needed – a round Second World War Pill-Box. There is something almost elegant about the way it was made out of cement-filled sandbags, but Grune Point was never invaded and it must have been a bleak position to man on a winter's night and it was a bleak night too in December 1956 when reports went out that a wildfowler had gone missing. It turned out to be a false alarm but four local firemen — there was no lifeboat station then at Silloth — went out into the waters of Moricambe Bay to look for him. All four were drowned and now there is a little cairn, shaped something like a janissary's hat, on top of the pill-box as a memorial to them.

Moricambe Bay always looks like a spelling mistake, but the better known Morecambe on the Lancashire coast did not officially come into being as a town until 1870 when the growing fashion for sea-bathing caused the village of Poulton-le-Sands to expand and swallow up its neighbours. It took on the name of the Bay, but this Moricambe – Latin for sea-bend – was the one mentioned by Ptolemy and so can claim precedence.

It forms a natural harbour and Edward I was one who recognised its strategic potential. In his wars against the Scots he could land supplies here for his troops in complete safety and shortly before his 1299 campaign the bay held as many as three dozen ships at anchor here. There is every chance that Skinburness could have become the major port along the whole of the Cumberland coast. In 1301 it was given the status of a free borough and then was granted a charter allowing a market to be held there once a week and an annual fair lasting seventeen days. But all this

St. John's, Newton Arlosh

promise came to an end three years later when the town was wrecked by a massive storm. We will never know what it was truly like all those years ago for the people of Skinburness, but in 1917 when a similar combination of an exceptionally high tide and onshore gale-force winds totally destroyed the little fishing village of Hallsands in South Devon, the villagers there did leave us an account of their ordeal. Terrified families were clinging to their doorframes as walls collapsed and floors fell away beneath them. One young woman described how "the roaring waves were bouncing over us, the rafters all breaking in. We could see the white waves foaming underneath the floors. The sea came down the chimney." It cannot have been much different in Skinburness seven centuries ago, except that there would have been no kind of government aid to help them.

They do seem to have tried to rebuild their lives and their homes, but a year later it is clear that they had given up and there is a request in the

the Pill Box at Moricambe Bay

Parliamentary Records for the fair and the market to be moved to Kirkeby Johan – the village now known as Newton Arlosh: the *New Town on the Marsh*. For the next two hundred years the monks of Holm Cultram faithfully served and cared for the new church of St John which was built there and it was certainly built to withstand attack. Along with St Michael's at Burgh-by-the-Sands, it is one of the finest examples of a fortified church in the whole of the Border area. Comparatively small though it is, hardly more than fifty feet in length, its walls are up to four feet thick in places, and the entrance, at only 31

inches, was clearly designed to allow no more than one person at a time to enter. And if any raider ever did manage to get in then the villagers were able to retreat behind an 8 inch thick door and up a spiral staircase into the tower. There was no way of getting into the tower through its windows either, as they were no more than slits, with the lowest at least seven feet from the ground.

But there is no way to defend against the ravages of time and neglect and little more than forty years after the dissolution, when there were no more monks to minister there, it was recorded that "...the Chapel of Newton Arlosh did decay; the door stood open and sheep lay in it. About fifteen years since the roof fell down, and the lead was taken away by some of the tenants and converted into salt pans." And that, it seems, is how it stayed for the next two hundred and fifty years and it was not until the middle of the nineteenth century that any attempt was made at restoration.

The Church Guide observes, and almost in passing, that "in 1843, thanks to the generosity of Miss Sara Losh of Wreay... and others, the church was restored and extended." Even apart from the misspelling of her name, this does scant justice to one of the most remarkable women of her generation. Sarah Losh (1785-1853) was by no means, as one might assume, a quiet and devout maiden lady who simply handed out money she had inherited from Daddy. She was an outstandingly gifted, self-taught architect, rightly referred to by Simon Jenkins in his *England's Thousand Best Churches* as "a Charlotte Brontë of wood and stone".

St Mary's at Wreay (pronounced *Wree-a*), a few miles south of Carlisle, a church which she designed and built herself between 1840 and 1842, is undoubtedly her finest achievement and though its location ought, strictly speaking, to put it outside my remit, I have to say something about it. And I have to urge you to visit it. Shaped like a Roman basilica, it is a memorial commemorating her beloved sister Catherine who had gone with her on a "Grand Tour" of Europe in 1817. And what a joyous memorial it is; everywhere inside there are symbols of light triumphing over darkness and of life overcoming death. There are ears of wheat and luxuriantly trailing vines; there are birds and there are butterflies. In the font, which Sarah carved herself, lotus flowers float on a mirror of "water" and time and again you come across pine cones, the

The Solway Firth

classical symbol of eternal life. It is a *Benedicite* of wood and stone, calling out "O all ye works of the Lord, bless ye the Lord" and it is not at all surprising to learn that Wordsworth had often been a guest in her father's house when she was young.

One of the hallmarks of Sarah's own work is her penchant for bog-oak. The pulpit itself is made from a stump so old it might even pre-date Christ himself and there are two lecterns, one an eagle and the other a pelican, which also stand on pillars of bog-oak. The same is true of the lectern in Newton Arlosh. It is hard to know now how much else in Newton Arlosh is her work, but the pale blue walls decorated with fleurs de lis in gold make it quite one of the most beautiful parish churches to be found anywhere. Outside, the stone eagle, symbol of hope and of everlasting life, perched high up on the roof over the original nave is certainly hers.

There is no trace or echo here now of those bands of marauding thieves, the Reivers. And yet, while Newton Arlosh itself is one of those quiet, pretty little villages, redolent of cucumber sandwiches and whist drives, I think even Miss Marple herself would be surprised to learn that in the late 1970's it had been home to a pair of serial killers. Their names were Archibald Thompson Hall and Michael Kitto. To begin with, Hall was only a petty criminal, as they were called in those days, when people wore flared trousers and had long hair. But during a stay in Parkhurst he had taught himself to talk *posh*. He used the prison library to read up on fine wines etc., learned to cook in the prison kitchen, and when he left, having written himself some glowing references, he began life again as a butler — robbing his employers of course as a sideline. In all respects it was proving to be a fine new profession, but things took a sudden and dramatic change when Kitto, his accomplice, clumsily killed one feeble, rich old lady in Knightsbridge. Dumping her body in the boot of their car, and with her ancient and gaga husband heavily drugged on the back seat, they drove north to Newton Arlosh, where Hall had rented a cottage.

At this point it becomes hard to keep pace with their exploits. They had been joined by Mary Coggle, also known as Belfast Mary, who was meant to take care of the murdered woman's husband, but he was proving difficult, so they beat him to death and took his body over the border into Scotland to bury it. Back again they went to Newton Arlosh, where Mary began drinking too much and talking on the phone too much. Clearly she was becoming a liability, so they bludgeoned her to death with the poker and threw her body into the river at Middlebie, a village just south of Lockerbie. It was then approaching Christmas 1977, and Hall spent the festive season with his younger brother Donald. When it was over they all went back to Newton Arlosh again where Donald, unfortunately, seems to have irritated the other two, so they chloroformed him and then drowned him in the bath. Into the boot he went and next morning, after Hall had taken a bath himself, they drove north. Hall, born in Glasgow, seems to have thought that Scotland was the right place to dispose of bodies, but bad weather caused them to spend the night in Berwick at the Blenheim House Hotel, with Donald's body still in the boot.

The manager of the hotel grew suspicious of them: too much blather and not enough luggage. He rang the police who checked and found that for some reason Hall had changed the number plates on the car they had hired, so they came to investigate. A body in the boot was not what they were expecting. Hall and Kitto were arrested, but even then Hall wasn't finished. He managed to escape through a toilet window of the police station and caught a taxi to Edinburgh. You couldn't film anything so patently far-fetched and foolish. But it wasn't long before he was recaptured. With a dead body in the car and Kitto ready to confess all, it was over. Kitto was given fifteen years and Hall life imprisonment without parole. Still the story wasn't quite finished though. The following Christmas some of the villagers in Newton Arlosh received Christmas cards from him. The man had a certain style, it has to be said.

Now that may not be the kind of story you expect to come out of Newton Arlosh, but then how many times have you heard on the television news some bemused member of the public saying, "I never thought anything like that could happen here." *Here* is just where it always does happen.

The village of Newton Arlosh may have been built to re-house the people of Skinburness after the great storm, but Skinburness itself did not disappear completely. Writing in 1955, Brian Blake described it as "a tiny hamlet of whitewashed cottages". They are still there those cottages, and they are still whitewashed, but you have to look hard to find them among all the new housing, some of which is really rather grand. There is a hotel there too which must have been very grand in its day. It has that kind of ornate clutter to its façade which makes you feel that at some time it was, or ought to have been called *The Majestic.* In the twenties and thirties, no doubt people drove here, or were driven, in motor cars with big headlamps. Boys wearing pill-box hats and tight uniforms would have carried in their leather suitcases and they would have dressed for dinner. Now it is called the *Skinburness Leisure Hotel* and on the day I had lunch there they had the same number of people eating as they had AA stars on the board outside. There was a poster in the window beside me advertising forthcoming events. One was billed as *Absolute Murder* and another, in aid of Breast Cancer Research, promised 'a Ladies Only fun-filled night with a hypnotist, a stripper and music.' I found it very hard to equate this with the tidy villas and bungalows which lined the long, narrow road into Silloth. Silloth itself may have come down a little, but at least it has preserved its dignity. Trippers, but no strippers. It came as no surprise at all to learn that it has since closed down.

As you first drive into Silloth, you know that there's something different about it. Ulverston, the market town I live in, has a central square, but it isn't square and each of the four roads leading out of it does a dog-leg within yards. They don't go straight. In Silloth the roads do and they are wide and they cross each other at right angles. It is a town that has not simply grown and developed haphazardly the way most small towns in the county have. It was planned; the grid-iron theory becoming a bricks and mortar reality very easily as there was nothing there to start with, nothing to hinder or obscure it. Silloth, as its name tells us, had been one of Holm Cultram's coastal granaries – a sea lathe – and up until the 1850's it had no more than a handful of houses.

What brought about the change were not social but economic factors. Trade was increasing and Port Carlisle, which had once seemed the answer to the area's transport problems, was a tidal harbour, and so could provide only limited access. It was not enough; a new approach to Carlisle was needed and so the Carlisle and Silloth Bay Railway and Dock Company came into being in 1856. But it was something of a financial failure from the outset. Looking back we can see that it was never likely to be anything else. Goods traffic was one thing, but why, a local paper asked, would the people of Carlisle want to go for a day out to what was little more than "a rabbit warren"? A fair question. So it was decided to turn the question on its head and transform the rabbit warren into a fashionable resort. It was a bold and calculated decision, the sort of decision one expects from Northern industrialists in the middle of the nineteenth century. A firm of Liverpool architects was employed and given the task of creating a totally new town. By 1857 forty houses had been built and on August 18th of the same year the foundation stone was laid for a new dock. It was a massive block of red sandstone into which was inserted a time-capsule, an oak box containing coins of the realm, copies of the Carlisle newspapers and plans for the new town and harbour. Fifteen hundred people had come from Carlisle, marching to the station behind bands and banners. Sir James Graham tapped the stone into place, two hundred and eighty guests sat down to a "substantial collation of fish, cold meats and game", and the navvies went on digging. They had started in April and had to shift half a million cubic feet of earth and rock. The site would cover four acres and the dock itself, when it finally opened two years later, measured six hundred feet by three hundred. And that is a lot of digging.

At the outset there were regular steamer services to Liverpool, The Isle of Man, Dublin, and Belfast and though the Belfast service was withdrawn in 1918, sailings to Douglas and Dublin lasted right up until 1943. There was an attempt to reintroduce the service in 1949, but before the year was out the crew were all caught smuggling and were arrested. Their vessel was impounded and so that was the end of that.

One of the legal imports from Ireland in the early days, however, was geese. They were shipped over in their hundreds and as soon as they were off-loaded they were led through a mixture of sand and tar so that they had nice thick shoes on their feet. They needed them too, as they were going to have to walk all the way to market.

John Ostle – the man with the pet barnacle goose – must have been a shrewd observer and not just of birds, as his diary entry for August 21st 1860, when the dock had only been open a year, reads, "At Silloth the dock looses water very fast. There is a diver goes down to stop the leak. They dare not let the water out of the dock for fear the sides fall in and then there would be a bad job." It held out for almost twenty years but in April 1879 there was indeed a very *bad job*. A low rumbling was heard, and then the west side of the dock wall collapsed, forcing open the gates. Within half an hour there were twenty-one vessels high and dry, or rather low and dry on the dock bed. To their credit, it took them only a week to free the trapped vessels and to decide that the best solution would be to build a second, and larger tidal dock behind the first one. Six more years of digging were followed by more crowds, and more banners. The first vessel to break the blue ribbon and sail in was the aptly called *Silloth*. A gun was fired from the forecastle, the people cheered and the Silloth Artillery Volunteers Band played *Rule Britannia* and there was another official lunch.

During all these years the town was developing. The grid-iron plan was complete. Six streets named after local rivers, Eden, Wampool, Esk, Caldew, Waver and Petteril ran down to Criffel Street. Now there were not only houses, there were shops and hotels; Silloth was becoming a resort. As Wood's 1885 Guide Book put it, "The merchant, manufacturer, tradesman, mechanic, and mill-worker – all hie hither, certain of joyous hours, pure air, refreshing breezes, and renewed health. The lustreless eye becomes bright, and the pallid cheek blooms anew."

The advertisements in the Guide give us a very clear picture of what it was like. There were tea and coffee merchants, grocers offering wines and spirits. The Queen's Hotel informed its visitors that "A Porter Awaits Every Train." You could hire a dog-cart or a pleasure boat. Wilson, Jespers and Co was the place to go for "Gentlemen's and Boys' Sea-side suits." And in Wampool Street was Longcake's Straw Bonnet Establishment. They didn't only make ice cream.

Perhaps most evocative of the times is J.D. Studholme's advert for The Silloth Baths:

These baths have been filled up regardless of expense, on purpose to secure the comfort and convenience of Bathers, the WATER BEING DRAWN FROM THE SEA by steam power, at the rate of 100,000 gallons every tide Each bath is a separate apartment, and on every occasion of use is filled with 100 gallons of pure salt water. Each Bath is supplied with two clean Towels and Brushes. The Ladies' Baths are under the supervision of Experienced female attendants.

It was open from 6 am to 10 pm and a bath — they were hot baths — cost 1/6d.

If you were more daring, you could hire a bathing machine on the sands and a horse would pull it into the water; Clean Towels and of course experienced female attendants were again available.

There was already a pier and soon there would be a promenade, a golf course, an Amusement Arcade and donkey rides. Looking back at old postcards and photographs, they seem to have been such innocent times, and never more so than in the pictures of the Pierrots with their white faces, baggy white costumes and white pointed hats with black pom-poms. *Dave Fuller and His Merry Men and Maids* they were called, and for thirty years they entertained holiday-makers with their daily open-air performances on The Green, 6d if you wanted a seat and 2d if you were happy to sit on the hill. I can't help thinking that today they'd be howled down, if not pelted with beer cans..

Margaret Forster remembers that in the 1950's Silloth was the only holiday resort worth going to – at least if you lived in Carlisle. Hordes of

43

families at Carlisle station would be struggling to get on the train, all laden down with buckets and spades – and they weren't plastic then but metal and lethal — and picnics. No hot-dogs to be bought then. No popping into the supermarket. You had to make your own sandwiches, wrap them up and take them with you, along with (let's be practical about this) your raincoat. Melvyn Bragg, living that much nearer, in Wigton, used to go by bus and he too remembers it as being the perfect place for a day out; there was an amusement arcade, donkeys, ice-cream and at the station there was a machine where you could punch your name out on a metal strip. He makes no mention of the Pierrots.

But my favourite story to come out of Silloth's musical past features the Choral Society. It was in the mid 1930's. They were due to give a performance of *The Messiah*, but they had not got a regular accompanist, so they were absolutely delighted to learn that the young wife of Bert Wilson, the new Bank Manager, gave piano lessons. They invited her to a rehearsal and were even more delighted when they heard how well she played. It is just a pity that they didn't ask her if she could sing, as Kathleen Wilson's maiden name was Ferrier and I can well imagine that the first few notes of *But Who May Abide the Day of His Coming* would have quickly had them sitting up straight in the Pavilion. I was glad to see that on the wall of the Nat West bank in Eden Street there is a plaque to her memory.

Times have changed since. There are caravan sites on the Skinburness Road, but Silloth is not the resort it was. The collapse of the pier and then Dr Beeching's closure of the railway line cannot have helped, but one of the problems is that there is still something a little Victorian about it. It has retained something of its graciousness and its respectability and maybe these are not qualities much in demand any more. On a sunny Sunday afternoon in August the crowds are all further down the coast in Allonby.

There is another thing which Silloth has retained and it seems quite ironic that a town which began as a granary should end up having quite one of the ugliest structures possible rearing itself up at the end of Criffel Street and only yards away from the elegance of The Green – Carr's Flour Mill.

The new and deeper harbour had opened up possibilities which the

Inside Carr's Flour Mill

Carr family were quick to recognise. Wheat from Canada and the Continent, needed for its higher gluten content, could now be shipped to Silloth directly, and in bulk. There was an abundance of local coal to power the machinery and a railway line to transport flour anywhere in the country. It was the perfect site and within a year of the opening of the harbour in 1885, the Carrs had built their first mill.

But that was not the beginning. Back in 1831 the founder of the dynasty, a Quaker miller, by the name of John Dodgson Carr, had walked the 51 miles from his home in Kendal to Carlisle to set up a bakery where his speciality was making biscuits. (With a thick slice of mature Cheddar Carr's *Table Water Biscuits* have long been among my favourites.) And to celebrate the 175th anniversary of that event the company recently launched *The Miller's Way,* a new long-distance footpath following the way he went, through the Howgills, Shap Fells and the Eden Valley.

In Silloth the company flourished and 1904 saw major extension work and the installation of the great Carel Steam Engine. A massive, twin-cylinder engine with an eighteen foot flywheel, its 700 horsepower drove all the machinery in the mill right up until 1973, and it is still there, but as befits such a faithful servant it has been retired to the museum, all shining valves, polished brass and enamel. Pure Fred Dibnah it is. I am told he once came to pay it a visit, and he loved it.

For nearly seventy years it had operated with no more than a handful of involuntary stops, one being when a cat had the misfortune to fall into the revolving flywheel. It was killed instantly of course, but centrifugal force pressed it against the inside of the flange and round and round it went, night and day, sixty-five times a minute for ten days, when what with the heat in the engine room the smell finally got too much for the engineers and they asked the manager to stop the mill. There were two minutes of silence, the cat's remains were extricated and cremated in the furnace of one of the boilers and the engine started up again.

If you look down the index of a road atlas, there is almost a full column of towns and villages whose names begin with *Mil* and clearly there must have been a time when every community of any size would have had its own wind or water mill. They could not have existed without them. At the end of the Second World War there were still almost 300 mills in Britain. Now the number is down to under 70. But if the days of Windy Miller are gone for ever, so are the days of Dusty Miller. Inside Carr's Mill everything is gleaming white and spotless, with pipes and tubes going everywhichway. I had not been prepared for anything quite so futuristic. And of course every aspect of the entire process is controlled and recorded by computer. But tradition is by no means lost at Carr's. Ben Clark, the Operations Manager, can trace his own family back through seven generations of millers and he has family records to show that back in the 1840's they were operating water and steam powered mills in London, but eventually size mattered and the last family-run mill closed down in 1993 in Soham in Cambridgeshire.

Almost every trade, industry and profession must have added something to the language, and I am not thinking simply of technical terms, but of expressions like *to fly off the handle,* or *to upstage* or *to earmark*, expressions which we have to consider carefully to realise where

Silloth Harbour

they came from and what they once meant. *It's all grist to the mill* means something you can turn to your advantage and make a profit from, but Ben explained that doing the very opposite of what that means in milling terms is how they have made their profit. *Grist* is grain and it was once the practice to mill several different types all together and hope that what resulted was near enough what you wanted – it was all flour. But at Carr's every different type of wheat is milled separately and then the different flours can be blended to produce a specialist flour for a specialist purpose, especially true of the Breadmaker Flour, for which they are famous.

If the mill was first built to capitalize on the port, the port now seems to depend largely on the mill. Of the hundred vessels a year which come into Silloth harbour, almost a third are bringing in wheat, and the only other imports are fertilizer from Russia and Africa, and molasses for the animal food firm, Caltech. But Silloth is also exporting live fish. Salmon smolt, bred at Armathwaite and Haweswater until they are about eight or nine inches long, are brought by road, transferred to ships fitted out with

Peeling the shrimps

tanks of fresh sea water and then off they go, as many as a hundred thousand of them, up to the fish farms in Scotland. Fish are not the only livestock they have handled at Silloth though. The Harbour Master, Captain Chris Puxley, still has fond memories of three hundred alpacas. They had been flown into Manchester from Chile and were kept for a four-month quarantine period in the port's lairage facility. "Delightful animals," he said they were.

Silloth is not one of the easiest harbours to get into or out of. Just before high water the flood tide running up the Solway meets a counter-current running inshore and the pilot (another of Capt Puxley's jobs) has to balance the two as the water changes direction across the dock entrance. Some tense moments there must be, bringing a 3000 tonne vessel between the jaws of those lock gates which are no more than 18 metres wide at the top.

But there is a fleet of little boats which bobs in and out of the harbour with no trouble at all. There may only be six of them but they nevertheless constitute a shrimp-fishing fleet second only to that in the Wash. There are three families now trawling for the Solway brown shrimps out of Silloth, the Bennetts, the Baxters and the Rays and depending on the weather they go out every day. It was Alf Bennett I met as he climbed up a slippery-looking iron ladder onto the quay. His boat the *Boy Bailey* (he has another called the *Jaana B*) had just come in with three sacks of shrimps and one of his sons was winching them up. About 120 kilos, he said. And they could not be fresher. They are cooked on the boat as soon as the nets are brought in. Sometimes they have to go out as far as fifteen miles and the thought of a cooker full of boiling water on a boat that's pitching about was one of the reasons I thought twice about his invitation to go out fishing with them. Another reason was the look of that ladder.

Once the shrimps used to be "picked", that is peeled, by women sitting around tables in their own kitchens, but now there are health and hygiene regulations to be met and all this is done in a smelly but scrupulously clean, white-tiled little room near the harbour. First the catch is sieved and sorted into three grades and the two smallest are peeled by a machine. One really has to admire a mind ingenious enough to invent a machine no bigger than a birdcage which can pick up six shrimps at a time and peel them. Just a pity that, as Alf told me, the mind belonged to a Dutchman. The largest shrimps are still peeled by hand, then re-cooked in a blend of butter and spices and "potted". And you can buy them on the internet. From trawler net to internet, I suggested.

I watched the women doing the picking and guessed that the tales told around that table weren't often about shrimps. I did ask one if she liked shrimps. If she ever ate them. She pulled a face. "Eat them? I can't even bear the look of them," she said. "Just the thought of putting one of them in my mouth… Oh, no. And I don't like prawns either." I asked how long she had been doing the job then. "Quite a while really," she said. An answer which seemed to bewilder us both.

Three:

Charles Dickens visits Cumberland. Allonby. The Ship Inn. Capt. Joseph Huddart. Salt. Crosscanonby. Maryport. The Roman Fort. Humphrey Senhouse. The port. Coal mines. Sunday Schools. Shipbuilding. Industrial decline. Nether Hall. Regeneration. The Roman Museum. Maritime Museum. The Aquarium. Colin Telfer.

In 1857 Charles Dickens and Wilkie Collins decided to take a short holiday together. As Dickens explained in a letter to his friend John Foster, it was to be an "expedition to out-of-the-way places. Our decision is for a foray upon the fells of Cumberland; I have discovered in the books some promising moors and bleak places thereabout." That he should have been

Above: The old chapel, Allonby

attracted by *bleak* places shouldn't surprise us. The result was *The Lazy Tour of Two Idle Apprentices,* his little-known Cumbrian travel book.

It has to be said that there is rather a strong anti-northern flavour to it from the very start. The further from London they travel, so "The temperature changed, the dialect changed, the people changed, faces got sharper, manners got shorter, eyes got shrewder and harder." The towns are of course as bleak as any southerner would expect them to be. Wigton is "one of the most dismal places ever seen by eyes." And the people are mostly boors. In Carlisle "… a young man advanced behind a young woman for whom he appeared to have a tenderness, and hinted to her that he was there and playful, by giving her (he wore clogs) a kick." Or they are buffoons and figures of fun. But there is a lot of fun in it, and some of it is aimed at themselves. They decide to climb "…a certain black old Cumberland hill or mountain, called Carrock" and set out from Hesket Newmarket with their innkeeper as a guide. Inevitably it rains, inevitably the mist comes down, and inevitably they get lost. Dickens breaks his compass. Their guide admits he hasn't been up there in years and they begin to wonder whether there isn't better walking to be had in London "where there are nice short walks in level public gardens, with benches of repose set up at convenient distances for weary travellers." And then Collins (Thomas Idle as he is called in the book) trips and falls while trying to cross a stream. He sprains his ankle and is *crippled.* They do manage to get back to their inn, but any more mountaineering is now out of the question. Instead Dickens (Mr Goodchild) consults his maps and guide books again and discovers that "the most delicious piece of sea-coast to be found within the limits of England, Ireland, Scotland, Wales, the Isle of Man, and the Channel Islands, all summed up together was Allonby." So off they go to Allonby.

There were moments when it did almost live up to expectations, when "the low flat beach, with its pools of water and its dry patches, changed into long bars of silver and gold in various states of burnishing." But their first impressions had not been promising. Canon Rawnsley tells us that Allonby at that time was the most popular watering-place of the élite of Cumberland, but as their carriage pulled up outside the Ship Inn, the most fashionable of all its seven inns, Mr Idle wondered aloud whether a watering-place could really consist of "five gentlemen in straw hats, on a form on one side of a door, and four ladies in hats and falls, on a form on another side of a door, and three geese in a dirty little brook … and a donkey running away." This donkey proved to be so much the chief public excitement at Allonby — it was always running away — that they later wondered if it wasn't supported at public expense. There was a shop and you could buy anything you wanted there, so long as it was a camp-stool or a child's wheelbarrow. There was a library too, but no sign of any books, and that ruinous brick loft with the ladder leaning up against it was the reading room. They stood it for a day or so. There was the sea and there were shrimps to be eaten, but one morning, looking out of the window and seeing the donkey running away again, Mr Goodchild turned to his companion with a solemn air and said, "This is a delightful little Inn, excellently kept by the most comfortable of landladies and the most attentive of landlords, but — the donkey's right!" And that was the end of their visit to Allonby.

I was glad to see that they are still very proud of their Dickens connection at The Ship these days. There is a plaque on the front to celebrate his stay and the dining room is called *The Dickens Dining Room,* with a full set of his novels (looking as though they've been read too) on the sideboard and coloured prints all round the walls. But there was one thing there you can be sure Dickens would have had something to say about and that was the clock on the mantle piece. It was working. It was ticking and the hands were going round, but for some reason it was displaying the time in San Francisco.

I had decided it would only be fair to stay at The Ship to see how things had changed, but my arrival could well have featured in *Pickwick Papers.* The barman who had taken my booking over the phone a few days earlier might well have written it down somewhere, but he certainly hadn't told anyone, so when I rang the door bell late one afternoon in October no one was expecting me. Much consternation. Lots of apologies and lots of rushing about. But what a fuss they made of me, this most comfortable of landladies and most attentive of landlords. That much had not changed a scrap. There was no donkey though. I had a room in the front as Dickens had (possibly his) and I kept looking out just in case. But no sign of one. And yet… As I'd driven into Allonby I'd noticed that a change that had been made to the road sign. We were still *Welcome* but two letters having been deftly removed we were now being asked to *Please d i e carefully.* Someone, it seemed, still wasn't too happy with the place.

And yet, on the other hand, you could, if you had a mind to it, take those selfsame words for a profoundly religious exhortation, one perhaps befitting the Quakers who had had such a profound influence on the area. The long, low building you see on the left hand side, North Lodge, is a Quaker alms house. It was built by Thomas Richardson, a London banker, as a second seaside home. He lived in the middle part of it and its two wings each had three little cottages, occupied rent free by "spinsters and widows over 60 years of age", each of whom was given an annual allowance of £5. A little further along is what was once their Meeting House. Of course the Quaker Movement was founded in Cumbria (well, Lancashire, as it was then) at Swarthmoor Hall just outside Ulverston and George Fox is known to have preached in Abbeytown as early as 1667. And there's a Quaker burial ground in Beckfoot, not far from Silloth.

The tiny Allonby Meeting House is a private dwelling now and very pretty, but I am not sure how I would feel about living in what had once been a church. "And in God's house for evermore My dwelling place shall be" was never meant to be taken literally. I suppose the quiet of Quaker meetings might have left behind some very peaceful vibes, but I don't think the same could be said of the Congregational Chapel on the corner a little way further down. That is a private house too now and a striking building it is, but the hell-fire-and-damnation sermons of some of the old Dissenters could well have left some very different echoes ringing around in it. No, I don't think I'd care for it.

Opposite the Chapel, on the seaward side of the road, are the ruins of what was once the Reading Room and Library. This must in its time have been one of the most imposing buildings in the whole of the town and is another example of Quaker generosity, Joseph Pease of Darlington having added over £1,000 of his own money to the £200 that had been raised towards it by public subscription. It was built in 1862 to the designs of Andrew Waterhouse who had also designed the Natural History Museum in London. It was a totally functional building, nothing decorative about it whatsoever. In fact, with its outside staircase to the first floor and its clock tower it has often been described as "railway architecture". But it was one of those warm-hearted, if paternal acts of nineteenth century benevolence aimed at the education of the "working man", and a writer in 1901 describes it as being "supplied with the best newspapers and magazines, and the shelves of the library are stored with numerous volumes in the various branches of science and literature." What happened to them all I do not know, but for the past thirty-five years it has stood empty and was rightly regarded locally as a total eyesore even before the great January storms of 2005 brought the chimney and tower crashing down through the roof. Allerdale Council were threatening to destroy it completely and perhaps one could hardly have blamed them if they had, but it has been bought by a couple who intend to restore it and live in it.

Alongside the Reading Room there was once the old tithe barn and the weaving sheds, and there still is an area known as Bleach Green where the newly-woven material was laid out in the sun. It is details such as this which help us to get a clearer picture in our minds of what life was once like in the little market towns of England. With Maryport some seven or so miles away and Silloth even further, Allonby had to be self-sufficient, which meant that as well as weavers and spinners it was also home to cobblers and tailors, carpenters and blacksmiths, cartwrights and wheelwrights, added to which there would be every kind of shop, the butchers and bakers, grocers and milliners, drapers and haberdashers, many of whose proprietors would have kept at least a cook and a housemaid. Then there would be the doctors and the clergy to look after them physically and spiritually. And in the larger houses of the profes-sional classes and the landed gentry there would have been menservants, coachmen and gardeners. There would have had to be a brewery (there is a Brewery Street) innkeepers, chambermaids and ostlers, while in the surrounding areas there would have been the farm labourers and the milkmaids, and the shepherds, the ploughmen and the carters. Everyone had a job to do. Well, nearly everyone. As always, there were a few rich enough to be idle and Allonby was somewhat out of the ordinary as it had decided it could profitably cater for these few. It became a resort and learned to indulge and pamper them. As Bulmer's *History & Directory of Cumberland* stated "The air of Allonby is highly salubrious and conducive to longevity, as the bills of mortality show." As well as its salubrious air, the town had the added advantage of a long, sheltered, crescent-shaped beach with a slope so gentle as to be perfect for those new horse-drawn bathing-machines which had become the fashion, and the beach being mostly shingle there was little danger of the wheels getting stuck or the horses sinking. But Allonby even went one stage further and in 1835 they raised £1,800 in £5 shares and built the Bath House. With stately columns on either side of its front door, it was, and still is a most elegant building and dominates *The Square*, even if it isn't actually a square at all, but an oblong and hardly more than twelve paces across.

As at Silloth it was 1/6d for a hot bath but you could, if you were brave enough, have a cold one for a shilling. Here too the Ladies' Baths were under the charge of experienced female attendants, but the Allonby adverts stressed that "Only pure Sea Water is kept on these premises." Which is remarkable in itself as the Bath House must be all of 150 yards from the sea, but these were the days of mechanisation and the water was first filtered through something that looked like a great pepper pot which stood at about half-water mark and was then pumped up to the house by a donkey engine.

Heading south, you are almost out of Allonby before you even catch sight of the parish church, described by Bulmer as "of a cruciform structure and probably one of the worst examples of churchwardens' architecture to be found in the county." I have never met the term *Churchwardens' Architecture* before, but I think I know what he means. *Functional* might almost be flattering. Grim and forbidding as any nineteenth century mill it is, and inside it is an equally plain, no-nonsense kind of place, and yet it is light and airy and does have a cared-for feel to it. All the kneelers are new and brightly decorated with doves and robins, brief commemorations and words of peace, and I was pleased to notice one very up-to-date one with a windsurfer embroidered on it. Allonby is very popular with windsurfers these days. And down by the altar there was a white pair picturing a bride and groom. A nice touch that.

On the wall to the left of the altar is a marble tablet to the memory of Captain Joseph Huddart and decorated with a globe and sextant. His was one of those great eighteenth century success stories. He had been born in Allonby in 1741, so never even had the benefit of the Library and

Reading Room, and although we do know that one of his teachers at Cockermouth was a keen astronomer, he had little more than the most basic of educations, yet when he died in 1816 The Times obituary claimed that "his knowledge of mathematics and astronomy ranked him in the class, if not upon the level with the first professors of these sciences." Self-taught in all things, he must have been a truly remarkable man. The many charts he produced, among them being the first reliable chart of the St. George's Channel, were only one reason for him being elected a Fellow of the Royal Society; he was also credited with having written one of the first-ever accounts of colour-blindness. It is the range of the abilities of men like Huddart which astonishes us today. He had no qualifications whatsoever as a civil engineer, yet was called upon as a consultant when improvements were planned for the harbours at Maryport and Whitehaven. His greatest achievement though was an invention which had a major influence at sea: a steam-driven machine to make a stronger and more reliable rope, "unrivalled in this or any other country" as The Times put it. This son of an Allonby farmer had become so famous by 1804 that he was invited to lay the foundation stone of the new East India Dock in London, and so there is no doubt about it; his son was right to spend £500 on his memorial. His father deserved it.

Going out into the churchyard I realised that another important local trade was that of the stone carver. Some of the headstones are quite massive, standing all of six feet high, and one of the tallest has writing, in small letters, on both sides. *Sacred to the memory*, it begins, *of John Sharp of Allonby, Master Mariner, who died at Kingston Jamaica, 6 April 1805, aged 48 years, and also of Betty his wife*. And on and on it goes, with more of the family, but time has worn away much of the sandstone. It would be the perfect place to read Gray's *Elegy*. There are obelisks and crosses and urns and great slabs of stone, but when you get to the end furthest from the church, in the modern part, every headstone is of the same regulation height and size, nothing more than two feet high. Mass produced, no trace of individuality. And no sign of a cross. Why, I do not know. Why should the symbol of the Christian religion be barred from a Christian churchyard? I read somewhere that it was acceptable for a child's headstone to have a Mickey Mouse on it, but not a cross.

Walking back towards the church I noticed some striking Norse surnames. Thornthwaite for one. And a few miles down the road at Crosscanonby, just outside the church door there is a stone hog's back Viking tomb, shaped to look like a little house of the dead.

But Crosscanonby can date its history far further back even than the Vikings. On the cliff top above the coast road is the clear outline of a Roman milefort. It was small – about 45 feet by 60 and garrisoned by no more than a dozen men, but these mileforts – this is number 21 – were an essential part of the Roman coastal defence system which ran from Bowness down to Ravenglass. And immediately below the fort are the remains of Crosscanonby's saltpans, which were in use here as far back as medieval times.

Nowadays we are being warned time and again about the danger of ingesting too much salt, but we can't live without it and when it was the only way of preserving meat during the winter it was essential. So much so that *salary* comes from the Latin word for the money paid to the Roman army so the troops could buy salt. The place names Salthouse, Salton, Salta, and Saltcoates show how important the industry was in this area and in many ways the location was obviously ideal for it. The coast line is low, there are wide areas of sand and not far inland extensive areas of peat for the fires. By 1536 Holm Cultram Abbey was operating twenty-one saltpans stretching from Saltcoates right up to the Border. Those monks never missed an opportunity to earn a groat.

As the salt content of seawater varies according to seasonal changes, a process called "sleeching" was introduced to produce a really concentrated brine. Salt-laden sand from just below high water mark was raked up and shovelled into a cobble-lined pit called a *kinch*. The *kinch* was lined with clay on top of which layers of straw were put in to act as a filter. Seawater was then poured repeatedly over the salted sand and the brine filtered into a cistern. When it was concentrated enough to float an egg, the solution would be slowly evaporated in iron pans to produce large salty crystals. And a slow and laborious business it must have been as the *kinch* would have had to be cleaned out every time it had been used. I was told that you can still see the remains of the brine pits on the seaward side of the road, but if they are there they must be buried beneath the undergrowth as I could find no sign of them.

The saltpans were owned by the Senhouse family of Maryport until the middle of the eighteenth century when the importation of mined salt brought the industry to a close. The workers' cottages were still standing and, it seems, still habitable until the 1960's. They were a piece of our history, but the council destroyed them in 1970 and now they have put up a plaque to explain what *used* to be there. Why is it, I wonder, that only the houses of the rich and the great are thought worth preserving? Workers' housing of this kind are just as much part of our history and would provide a timely corrective to those paintings by the likes of Helen Allingham, paintings of peasants in their spotless smocks, standing outside their cottage doors and smiling among their hollyhocks.

The Senhouse family owned more than simply the Crosscanonby saltpans; they could at one stage be said to have owned the whole of Maryport and it was certainly they who named it. The settlement – there is nothing else one could realistically call it – which existed before they took an interest in the area was called Ellenfoot, taking its name from the river which rises in the Caldbeck Fells and flows down through Ireby, Torpenhow and Aspatria. But this Ellen is not a girl's name. In a Holm Cultram Abbey charter it is referred to as the Alne, which would suggest it was named after the Roman fort Alauna.

In its day Alauna was a major fortification, not just a Roman milefort. It covered over six acres, and housed more than a thousand infantrymen – the First Cohort of Spaniards – as well as some 250 cavalry. The site was perfect, commanding as it does an uninterrupted view of the Solway, the Scottish coast (Maryport is nearer to Scotland than it is to Keswick) and clear stretches of land away to the east. There could be no covert invasion or infiltration along this part of the coast. It was early in the second century that the fort was built and to judge by the coins found there it was occupied continually until the legions effected a complete withdrawal 300 years later. Once they had left, the *vicus*, the local civilian establishment servicing the camp and living on its outskirts, looks to have packed up and gone too. There must have been nothing to keep them there, and the next we hear of it at the beginning of the eighteenth century Ellenfoot still comprises no more than one small farmhouse and a few impoverished shacks down by the waterside, lived in by half a dozen fishermen who were also possibly engaged in a little part-time smuggling.

It was Humphrey Senhouse (1706-70) who brought about the changes. The family had opened their first coal mine, the Ellenburgh Colliery, in 1740 and he realised that if they could acquire a port then they could emulate and even rival the Lowther family's position of dominance in Whitehaven. He did not have the funds to undertake the scheme himself, but he managed to gather together a group of fifty-three co-trustees and a Bill was entered in Parliament for the "Repairing, Enlarging and Preserving the Harbour of Ellenfoot in the County of Cumberland". Royal assent was granted in 1748 and Humphrey celebrated by re-naming the port after his wife Mary. No, it was not, as one guide book affirms, named after Mary Queen of Scots, even though she did set foot briefly on the Cumberland coast. Even then it was in Workington, not Maryport.

Coal was brought down from the Ellenburgh colliery in panniers on the backs of donkeys and ponies to be exported to Ireland and it was not long before the area began to prosper and there were as many as seventy ships registered to the port, some as large as 300 tons. By 1752 we hear of a blast furnace and then of a glassworks, a paper mill, a pottery, and of a brewery. Maryport was beginning to be a town of some importance. We can best appreciate the changes that had taken place from the stately, if rather cumbersome Preamble to a Second Act of Parliament obtained in 1756.

"And whereas at the time of passing the former Act (of 1749) there was only one farm house with the outhouses and offices thereto and belonging, standing and built near the said Harbour of Ellenfoot, but in consequence of, and under the encouragement given by that Act, a great number of houses, warehouses and buildings have been erected and built adjoining or nearto the said Harbour on both sides of the River Ellen, and a great many trading persons have been encouraged to settle there and several useful manufacturers introduced and exercised and a considerable trade and commerce in iron, potters ware, glass, cordage, and fish and other wares and merchandise settled and established in the said place, so as to constitute and render the same a considerable town of trade, and the said town hath not yet obtained any determinate name or denomination, it is enacted and declared that the several houses and buildings now erected and built and to be erected and built, contiguous, near or adjoining

Maryport Harbour

the said Harbour on either side of the River Ellen shall from henceforth be called, known, and distinguished, together with the said Harbour, by the name and denomination of Mary-Port in all grants, pleadings, courts and places whatsoever."

It had a new name and had become "a considerable town of trade" in less than a decade. Busy port though it was though, it still had no lighthouse at this time and it is said that William Curry (I wish I could claim a family connection) used to hang a lantern in his shop window to guide the shipping. Later he hung it up outside on a pole.

Considerable trade meant that there was a considerable amount of money about. Architects and town planners now existed and the Senhouse family made wise use of them. Their new town was also designed and built to a grid-iron plan and much of its Georgian elegance, especially around Fleming Square, is still evident today. But there is another side to this wealth and elegance and that is the workforce which provided it. The population had grown to 1300 by 1774. By 1790 eleven new pit shafts had been sunk and in 1794 there was a cotton mill employing as many as 500 workers, but sadly, what we need to remember is that at this time many of those workers would have been children and they would not have been living or working in Georgian, or any other kind of elegance.

Maryport Harbour

Children brought up on farms had probably always helped out at home from the moment they could walk – feeding the chickens, scaring birds away from the corn and so on, but the advent of industrialisation meant a population movement away from the countryside and into the towns. It meant factories, mines and mills, and it meant that children as young as eight years old were sometimes kept working from 6 am until 8 pm. And in appalling conditions. In the mines they either carried coal on their backs or they sat in the dark and the damp opening and closing doors as they heard the wagons approaching. Brutal beatings seem to have been commonplace in the mills when tiny children could not keep pace with the machinery and as many of them were paupers taken from the orphanages they had no one to complain to, even had they dared. It was not until 1842 that Parliament made it illegal for boys under the age of ten to be employed underground.

We have no reason to believe that conditions in Maryport were any different. What we do know for certain though is what life was like for these little ones, and probably the rather better-off little ones, on the Sabbath. The Sabbath did not mean a day of rest for them. It meant Sunday School and the Rules and Resolutions are all there in the Minute Book of the Committee of Management. School started at 7am, but 8 in winter, and they were instructed in reading until it was time for divine service. It does not say how long this service lasted but we know they never tended to be short. The pupils were then briefly dismissed so they could go home for their dinners and then they were back again at 1.30 when they were given further instruction until the evening service at 3 pm. After that it was back yet again to be taught the catechism or any other plan of religious instruction until 7 o'clock. The masters were urged to be "particularly attentive to the morals and behaviour of their scholars and to take care that they come clean and decent to school and be regular in their hours of attendance and also to see that they go orderly and quietly to their several homes." And then to bed as they had to be up early for work on Monday morning.

Maryport's prosperity did not last however and the first slump came about early in the nineteenth century, largely as a result of the war against France. European ports had been blockaded and trade with America suffered too. The cotton mill went bankrupt, the glassworks and many other smaller manufacturing concerns were closed down and hundreds were unemployed at a time when there were no "benefits". Food became scarce. Bad weather had resulted in bad harvests and rising prices. In some years it went the other way and it was a case of drought and water shortage bringing the mills to a stop. In the winter of 1817 the women of Maryport had had enough. There were bread riots and troops had to be sent in to restore order.

But the failure of these heavy industries slowly began to be compensated for by the rise in ship building. The little fishing boats known as Allonby Wherries had been made in Maryport almost from the first days of its existence as a town, and the first actual shipyard, near to St. Mary's Church at North Quay, was opened in 1765 by William Wood of Whitehaven, his first ship being the 106 ton brig the "Sally". By 1794 ninety ships had been built there and there were as many as 200 carpenters at work. Other yards were to follow. First John Peat's on the south west bank of the Ellen and then later and a little further upstream where the paper mill had once been, the brothers Joseph and Isaac Middleton set up business in 1810. With great biblical names like that it seems only right that they should have been the founders of a shipping dynasty, and they were: Joseph was the great-grandfather of Thomas Henry Ismay, founder of the White Star Line which built the *Titanic*.

In 1838 it was decided that ships built at Maryport no longer had to be registered at Whitehaven; Maryport was now a port in its own right. But it was John Ritson who transformed the industry. Once a manager at Peat's, he began to build on his own account in the 1820's and when his sons came of age and joined him they built Maryport's first iron vessel. We can see how much things had changed: William Wood's first brig the *Sally* had been 106 tons, now, eighty years, later Ritson's *Ellenbank* was 1426 tons. One problem of this increase in size was that the River Ellen was far too narrow to allow such vessels to be launched in the conventional manner. It was only sixty feet wide and they would have simply impaled themselves on the opposite bank. So they had to enter the water broadside, a method which had been introduced by John Peat in 1837. What an occasion it must have been. The launch site, which can still be seen, was directly opposite Mote Hill which rises straight up to about 130 feet and so provided a perfect grandstand. Crowds of people would gather there and when the moment of high tide was reached, the signal would be given for the struts holding the vessel to be knocked away. The carpenters who did that job must have had to move pretty smartly then as it began to slide towards the water gathering speed all the time until it tumbled into the river. Three rolls were the average, the first one being well nigh rail to rail. None ever turned over though. Just imagine the noise, but imagine too the tidal wave it would have whipped up. It is said to have gone right across the road and up the hillside, catching out those who had thought they might get a better view from lower down and flinging them off their feet.

Prosperity had returned to the town. The 1856 register records ninety-one master mariners living in Maryport, many of them in the area of Fleming Square. The increase in trade called for new and better docks. The Elizabeth Dock, named after Elizabeth Senhouse, was opened in 1857 to be followed by the Senhouse Dock in 1884. As many as two hundred vessels could be in port at any one time and it has often been claimed that if you were nimble enough you could cross from one side to the other by jumping from ship to ship. But they had made one disastrous error when they designed the new dock. The dock gates were only 46 feet wide, which was ample for the conventional clippers which had an average beam of thirty-five feet, but the new steam ships were twice that width.

And just as the manufacturing industries had failed in the early years of the nineteenth century, so in the years before the First World War there was a decline in ship building. One of the reasons for this was because Maryport could only build the hulls; they could not build the engines or the boilers, so vessels had to be towed to the Clyde or the Tyne to be fitted out at the bigger yards. As the economic situation worsened, firms such as Ritsons could not be expected to compete with the likes of Swan Hunter or Harland and Wolff. The *S.S. Silverburn* was the last vessel to be built at Maryport and it was not even big enough to need a Maryport broadside launch, but went down the slipway prow-first. This was on 8th August 1914 and all that was left for the dockside ironworks then was to make shell casings for the wholesale slaughter that was about to come.

There were food riots again in January 1917. Prices of even basic foodstuffs had risen beyond the reach of many poor families. There was scarcity, it is true, but there was also profiteering and so the government had announced that it would fix prices, but in Maryport market, a farmer declared that he didn't care what the government said, that he'd charge whatever price he liked, and all hell broke out. Women rushed the stalls and carts and according to one report "the street was filled with hooting and yelling woman, while potatoes, cabbages and turnips went flying through the air." No doubt order was restored in the usual way and people went on being hungry.

There is a marked contrast between that famous post-war slogan about "a land fit for heroes" and the back-to-back houses we know they were living in. These were the houses described for us by D.H. Lawrence, and George Orwell and more recently by Roddy Doyle. The two-up-two-down houses with the one cold water tap in the kitchen. The dreadful overcrowding. The communal lavatories in the back yards. The bare feet. The zinc bath on the nail. This was the reality.

And things were to get worse. The miners strike of 1926 brought trade in the port to a standstill. In one week in June of that year the Relief Committee of Maryport handed out 890 food vouchers: 10/- for a wife and 3/- for a child. They could be exchanged in the shops for food. But it was not exactly charity; these were loans and the money would all have to be repaid. Men on strike received nothing of course and when the miners tried to hold a concert to raise some money for "the alleviation of distress" the Maryport Magistrates turned down their application.

Their endurance is hard to believe. It is the suffering in Jarrow that is remembered and their hunger march to London, but conditions in West Cumberland were every bit as bad. The Jarrow miners had one big advantage over their west coast brothers and that was the A1, a direct route south. If the miners of Cumberland had marched south they would had a problem which way to go once they got to Millom. The isolation of this part of the country has always been one of its main handicaps. It was far enough away from the government in London to be ignored. No one came to their help and by the 1930's 80% of the men in Maryport were unemployed. Yet there seems to have been a resilience there, a resilience of the kind which the Queen Mother looks to have recognised when she visited the north east in July 1936 and wrote in her diary of "a horrible scene of desolation, driving through crowds of emaciated, ragged, unhappy and undaunted people who gave us a wonderful reception. It made me weep — their courage is so high."

The decline can be seen in the buildings too. Or rather not seen. Many of the buildings which were once there have gone now. Looking at old photographs and postcards, one of the most astonishing is the railway station. Built in 1860, it was on a par with that in Carlisle, on a truly grand scale with a clock tower and pitched roof and all in handsome red sandstone. There were waiting rooms, one for ladies and one for gentlemen, for first class and third, a ticket office, company offices, a stationmaster's house and even a company Board Room. It was a major source of employment. There were drivers and firemen, guards and station staff. The fitting sheds alone employed 200 men. At the turn of the century it was carrying close on 12,000 passengers a week and including freight and goods traffic was taking well over £2,000. Now, if you want to take a train to Carlisle or Barrow, there is no station there at all, just a platform, not even anyone to sell you a ticket. You have to wait in one of those little glass-sided bus shelter affairs and it's unlikely you'll have anyone to talk to.

And then there was, but now there isn't, Ewanrigg Hall, the seventeenth century home of the Christian family, though Fletcher Christian, by far its most famous and once its most infamous member, was not born there but at a farm called Moorland Close near

Cockermouth. It has often been claimed that he somehow managed to get back from Pitcairn and is buried in the family tomb at Brigham, but there is no proof of that. In its day Ewanrigg Hall was grand enough and atmospheric enough for Wilkie Collins to have based Limmeridge House on it in *The Woman in White*. But it burned down in 1903 and that was the end of that.

Totally bizarre though and totally symptomatic is the story of Nether Hall, the Georgian home of the founders of Maryport, the Senhouse Family. (Fletcher Christian's grandmother was a Senhouse.) For four centuries it passed down through the family, down through a long succession of Humphreys until 1903 when the last of them died and his son, called Guy this time, inherited it. A military man, Guy Senhouse rose to the rank of Colonel and was regarded locally as a *gentleman*. However, he was the last of the family to live in the Hall and as he never married, when he died in 1952 the estate passed to his brother Roger. Now Roger was what was called in those days a *confirmed bachelor*. In fact he was Lytton Strachey's last lover, a member of the Bloomsbury set, the translator of Collette, and one of the founders of the publishing firm of Secker and Warburg. Maryport must have seemed to him like another planet. He had no intention whatsoever of living *there*. He sold off the farms and closed up the Hall. But while *he* may have had no interest in the Hall, some of the locals certainly had and before long it was broken into and systematically looted. Almost anything which could be carried off – and we are talking here of valuable pictures, silverware, furniture, books, coin and stamp collections — was carried off. There are stories too of local youths fighting "duels" out on the lawns with ceremonial swords they'd taken down off the walls. Then the vandalism started. By the time Roger died in 1970, bringing to an end 442 years of family history and possession, the place was a total wreck and a fire eventually finished it off in 1973. There was no insurance cover and the council demolished what was left standing. Now all that remains apart from the stables, is the ancient and stately Pele Tower and a few square inches of blue and white tiles where the entrance hall once was.

It must have come as a something of a shock and certainly a mixed blessing to Roger Senhouse's grand nephew, Joseph Scott Plummer, to find that as the only direct descendant he was now Lord of the Manor and had inherited this ruin and a derelict harbour. The harbour itself had almost totally silted up and the surrounding area was a waste land. The only saving grace, so I was told, was that the weeds had grown so tall they were now hiding the worst of it. With only a few sheds being used by local fishermen, it must have begun to look more and more as it had in the early eighteenth century when it was still Ellenfoot.

No one would have blamed Joseph if he had ignored it and stayed in London. He realised that there was nothing he could do by himself so he sold the harbour — I believe for £1 — to a consortium of English Estates North, Allerdale District Council and Cumbria County Council, who between them set up a design team in 1986 to work on a plan for the redevelopment of the whole area. The plan they came up with was as magnificent as it was ambitious and perhaps it could never have been achieved, but if it had been, Maryport would now have a Piazza with craft shops and a covered market, a leisure centre which would double as a sports and concert hall, and an elegant Maritime Heritage Building. Of course none of this exists, but what they did achieve is remarkable enough. The harbour has an identity of its own. The distinctive waterfront housing is extraordinarily attractive and the people who live there must have glorious views. It is an altogether delightful area to walk about in now and the Marina, with 161 berths, is always full of small boats and is clearly thriving.

The town does have two museums: the Maritime Museum and the Roman Museum. The Roman Museum is a little to the north of the harbour and on the site of the fort of Alauna. Looking at the shallow ditches and the grass-covered mounds today it is very hard to imagine what it must have been like when it housed those thousand infantrymen, though a visit to Aldershot or Catterick would probably tell us. Apart from the armaments and equipment, army life probably hasn't changed that much. And yet in one respect the officers of the second century Twentieth Legion were very different from today's Sandhurst men. When their commander, Claudius Albinus, led them back across the Channel to foster his own personal ambitions to seize power in Rome, they knew that their base would be vulnerable to attack and so, for safety's sake, they buried their personal *altars*. Some were discovered by John Senhouse late in the sixteenth century. Camden saw them in 1599 and described how Senhouse "a very honest man in whose grounds they were digged up, keepeth (them) charily and hath placed orderly about his house." Then in the nineteenth century when some deep ploughing was being carried out to the north-east of the camp they discovered seventeen more, the greatest single find of Roman inscriptions ever made in this country.

Joseph Scott Plummer has made the collection available for public display and they are now housed in the Old Battery which was built in 1885 to train gunners for the R.N.V.R. Sadly, I have to say that I find it all a bit disappointing. It is called the Maryport Roman Museum and I was expecting rather more than twenty or so big stones and a dozen smaller ones, no matter how fascinating the inscriptions, which are in Latin of course, may be to archaeologists. It is so very lifeless. I like my history to be more human. Give me the Jorvik Centre every time with its sounds and its smells.

The Maritime Museum is more varied and informative, but it is largely made up of photographs and display boards and again I would value more *things*. One thing it does have is Fletcher Christian's sea chest. But on my way home I started to wonder. If it *was* his sea chest, why hadn't he taken it to sea with him? Why wasn't it on the *Bounty?* And if it was on the *Bounty,* why didn't it end up on Pitcairn rather than Maryport? Some questions it is probably better not to ask; they only spoil a good story.

The Town Council has done its best to keep the Fletcher Christian link, or myth, alive. There is Christian Street, Fletcher Crescent, Bounty Avenue and Pitcairn Crescent and there is one other 'relic' in the town, in the Aquarium, a carving of a flying fish which it claimed was made out of a fragment of timber taken from the *Bounty*, but as the *Bounty* was deliberately burned this seems to come into the same dubious category as the sea chest.

There is nothing dubious about the Aquarium itself though and yet the story of how Mark Vollers came to open it does have its surprises. After graduating in marine biology, he and a friend teamed up in Anglesey to form a company selling seafood — primarily shellfish — to local hotels and restaurants. It was doing well, but Mark noticed that after they had bought what they wanted, many of the customers who came to the depot would often stay on, fascinated by the tanks where the live crabs and lobsters were kept, and he reasoned that if they were that interested then perhaps they could be persuaded to pay to see them, so they installed some more tanks and it was not long before the cash-flow from this scheme outpaced the shellfish market and a full-scale aquarium soon followed. That was in 1995 and since then Mark has designed six more, coming to Maryport in 1997.

I have always loved going to aquariums, but this one is special. It calls itself a coastal aquarium, yet the first thing you meet as you go in is a small tank of minnows, the sort of freshwater fish you'd see in a little steam and then as you move along so this "stream" gets bigger and there are sticklebacks, then carp and perch. Then the stream reaches the Solway Firth and the salt marshes, where mullet and bass spawn. And there are rock pools with star fish in them and sea anemones and hermit crabs. And then at last we reach the sea itself. My favourite tank is the big, open one where the plaice and the rays are. The plaice can shuffle down into the sand, change colour if need be and disappear, while the thorn-backed rays have brown patterns on them as intricate as any Persian carpet. When they swim up to the sides of the glass and you see their white undersides – their faces – they are so spooky. They remind me of those 'ghosts' you'd see in comics like the Dandy and the Beano.

Elsewhere you have the illusion of being under the sea itself, one tank being inside the ribs of a 'sunken wreck'. Mark Vollers has an imagination as well as practical skills. It is a total delight and of course these days you are going to see far more fish there than you are likely to see landed on the harbour side. During the depression years it was the fishermen who kept the harbour open, but there are hardly more than half a dozen boats operating out of it on a full-time basis now.

Time was, they tell me, when fishermen would sit on those chains that hang between the dumpy concrete posts that line the edge of the harbour. They would sit there with a few strings of fish to sell, and their mates might come and stand alongside them for a bit of a crack and maybe a little lad out with his dog would stop by and listen to them, hoping for a bit of fish – the dog certainly would be. Yes, time was when such things were an everyday event down at the harbour, and now that very same scene has become an event for every single day, as it is the scene that sculptor Colin Telfer has re-created for us here, life-size and so life-like

Colin Telfer at work.

that if it were not or the fact that the figures are as red as iron ore you'd very likely find yourself stopping to join in the conversation. You'd maybe even try to buy some fish.

Colin Telfer is simply one of the most remarkable men I have ever met. Born in the little mining village of Fothergill, his only early education was at nearby Flimby where he remembers they mostly wrote on slates, but sometimes he was given a bit of paper to draw on as the teacher recognised he seemed to have a talent for it. But at fifteen he left school. No time for drawing now. Like the rest of the lads in his class he went to work in the mines, not underground though. First he was a 'token boy' identifying who'd filled which tubs of coal as they came up to the surface, then in the 'tippler house' which was freezing cold most days of the year, until, in his early twenties, he became a winding engineman, a position of such responsibility and respectability that earlier generations had come to work in bowler hats, collars and ties and with watch chains spread across their ample waistcoats.

Colin Telfer and "Selling the Fish", Maryport Harbour

Then one day something happened to change his life. His wife Maud threatened to spend good money on a painting of the Packhorse Bridge at Ashness to hang on their sitting room wall. Colin, who, as he says himself, had had a few at the time, insisted he could do one himself and just as good. And he did – with house paints – his brother was a decorator. But it didn't stay on the wall for long; someone bought it. He carried on painting — scenes of Maryport — and locally his reputation grew. Every painting he ever did after that was bought and sadly he never thought to take any photographs of them.

But he still had a living to earn and for twenty years he went on working in the mines, moving from one pit to another as they closed down and the industry slowly dwindled to its death. Harrington was the last – he worked in the winding-house there – and that was the end of it; there were no more pits to work in. He considered himself lucky to get a job with British Steel, even though he hated it, but that lasted no more than three years. Another closure. More men unemployed.

But British Steel were, to their credit, offering re-training schemes. These were fine so long as you wanted to drive heavy-goods vehicles or be an upholsterer, but *Telf,* as his friends in Maryport call him, decided that if he could paint then he could be a sign-writer and earn his living that way, so he enrolled for a course at Carlisle College of Art.

Initially he was expected to try his hand at everything: photography, life drawing, print making and so on, but it was the sculpture class that caught his imagination. The trouble was that it was a two-year course and British Steel were only funding him for one. At this point in the story we have to recognise the enormous debt which Cumbria owes to his wife, Maud. It was she who told him that if he didn't go ahead with it he would regret it for the rest of his life. They could manage, she insisted, on his redundancy money and the dole, but as his dole money was £25 a week and his fares to Carlisle were £15 it can't have been easy.

Colin's break-through came when he was looking out of the train window one morning on the way to the College and saw an old coal tub near a worked-out mine, and he realised that what he should be concentrating on were the things and the experiences of his own life. And so he began making little figurines from memories of his childhood in the pit village: children playing marbles, his mother at the dolly tub or making a hooky mat. And of course the miners themselves. The figures were resin-based but what made them special was Colin's realisation that if he were to mix coal dust into the resin they would look to have been actually carved out of coal. Not surprisingly these figures sold and sold, but his major break-through came in 1992 when the Egremont Heritage Trust commissioned him to make a life-sized sculpture of an iron-ore worker pushing a tub. This time he used iron-ore dust instead of coal to give the work that distinctive red tone.

This was the beginning and now, as we will see as we move on south, his work is to be found in every coastal town from Maryport to Barrow. They are such fine pieces of work too, with such a distinctive style and what I admire is not only the practical skill that has gone into the making of them but the thought behind them. As he once said while walking round a piece he was working on in the clutter of his yard in John Street, "It needs a good dose o' looking at to get it right. There's 90 percent looking and 10 per cent doing." And what eyes for looking he has. I am reminded, in the kindest way, of those lines in *Julius Caesar* when Caesar says of Cicero that he has "such ferret and such fiery eyes." When Telf looks at you, you know you are being looked at.

Four:

Flimby. Helen Craik. Workington. The Curwen family. Coal. John Christian Curwen: MP, industrialist and agriculturalist. Irish immigrants. Mining disasters. Strikes. Iron works. Henry Bessemer. Miners' living conditions. Helen Thompson. Workington Hall. Portland Square. Finkle Street. Mary Queen of Scots. St Cuthbert. St Michael's Church fire. Edmund Blood. Bill Shankly.

You don't have to travel far down the road towards Workington before you come across another piece of Colin Telfer's work. Less than two miles in fact. It is shortly after the *Welcome to Flimby* sign and at the

Edmund Blood's "St. Cuthbert" in Workington Parish Church

entrance to the Risehow Industrial Estate, but, if you pushed him, Colin would probably say it isn't in Flimby or Risehow either — such is the rivalry that still exists between the old pit villages — but in Fothergill, which is where he was born. Appropriately, as it is very close to the first mine he worked in, it consists of the half circle of a pithead winding gear and two miners sitting down and having a smoke and a chat. It is the animation on their faces that catches you. These men are *talking*. And they've just been joined by a third man swinging his miner's lamp.

Flimby was a brilliant place to grow up in, Colin Telfer says. He and his friends cooked winkles on the beach and were regularly chased through the trees by the Sheriff of Nottingham, but it has a grim look to it now. I know you can't really judge a place unless you live in it, and it does have the Flimby Male Voice Choir and a Silver Saxhorn Band, but all the eye can see are rows of featureless houses with many of the older ones all boarded up. And in the churchyard the early headstones have been rooted up and leaned against the wall, which is a pity as I was hoping to find the grave of Helen Craik, who died there in 1824, but I could find no trace of it. The pity of it is that hers is a story almost as Gothic as the novels she wrote while she was living in Flimby Lodge.

But she wasn't born in Flimby. She was born at Arbigland in Dumfries, the daughter of William Craik, a rich, powerful and respectable landowner and in her early life she wrote poetry skilful enough to win praise from Robert Burns himself; in fact it is a celebratory poem of hers and in her own handwriting which appears at the beginning of the famous Glenriddel Manuscript, an autograph volume of Burns' poems which he transcribed for their mutual friend Captain Robert Riddel. But then, free spirit that she seems to have been, she 'formed an attachment', as the saying was, with one of her father's grooms. There were clandestine meetings, and when her family found out about them there was of course one almighty row. The groom, by the name of Dunn — we don't even know his first name — seems to have known nothing of what had happened, as he went off, apparently not suspecting anything, on an errand to Dumfries. Not long afterwards his horse came back, but riderless and Dunn, surprise, surprise, was found dead. He had been shot not far from the entrance to the estate. The locals cried murder, but the Procurator Fiscal brought in a verdict of suicide. The Craiks were influential people.

Not people to be messed with and certainly not by grooms.

Helen was never seen at Arbigland again, though in later years the ghost of a lady in white was sometimes glimpsed near the spot where the groom had died. In a poem *Lines Written in the Summerhouse at Arbigland, Feb 25, 1752* she bewails her fate and insists that she is guiltless. Nevertheless she was banished to the house of her Uncle James Craik at Flimby, and her poems, once bright and cheerful, began to show an increasing predilection for suicide and murder. A friend was moved to complain:

> With powers so great how could you, Helen,
> So hideous a subject dwell on?

Perhaps fortunately for her, those were the very years when suicide and murder were the stock-in-trade of the fashionable Gothic Horror Novels — running into three or four volumes and often totalling as many as a thousand pages — and Helen contributed to the genre with titles like *The Hermit's Cell* and rather more salaciously *The Nun and her Daughter*. I suppose every headstone is covering some story worth listening to.

Flimby Lodge, where she lived, became a Ladies School for a while and then was bought in 1886 by the Cockermouth Union to be converted into a workhouse school. Even as late as 1914 it was still housing 31 boys and 14 girls. How many of those boys were still alive at the end of the War it would be interesting to know.

If Flimby is grim, the wind farm that lines the road towards Workington is a horror, but with nothing Gothic about it. It looks like a deliberate affront, as though the authorities had decided that in an area like this it really doesn't matter what you do. After all it's only Workington.

Workington. It is a name likely to strike fear into the heart of any southerner. A name that calls up images of iron and steel and coal, cloth caps and horny-handed sons of toil, the very grime out of which the industrial revolution was spawned. It could be an allegory, a name invented by Dickens or Samuel Butler. And the simple truth that it is derived from a Saxon settler with a name something like *Weorc*, and that it was where his *ton* or farmstead was, will never change any of that. Workington is stuck with its name and, I suspect, with the fact that many of our gut feelings, even when we are not southerners, turn out to be not so very far from the truth.

When Dorothy Wordsworth passed through the town in 1828 on her way to the Isle of Man, the only thing she wrote in her journal was, "Workington very dismal. Frightened in the streets." And she was no scaredy-cat, Dorothy.

There are no archaeological remains to tell us anything about *Weorc*, his farmstead or his kinsfolk, but this is hardly surprising, given the growth of the town, with its seven major iron and steel works and its 180 foot high spoil heaps. Nor is there any trace of the Vikings, who, driven out of Dublin in the early tenth century, are thought to have come here peacefully and settled down among the Saxons. And there is no mention of Workington in the Domesday Book; the Normans, it seems, took their time getting up here. Well, there was nothing for them really.

The first name to step out of the fog of history is Patric de Culwen, the precursor of the Curwen family which was to dominate the area for centuries to come. The earliest example of the Curwen coat of arms is on a wax seal of 1257 and about that time Patric it was who moved the family home from Burrow Walls to the present site at Workington Hall. His grandson, Gilbert, fought at the Battle of Falkirk, where Edward I defeated "Brave Heart" Wallace. The family history has it that it was his arrival on the scene which changed the course of the battle and when it was all over he is said to have boasted to Edward "Ah, where would you have been if I had not been there!" And part of that boast "Si je n'estoy" (No aristocrat spoke English at that time) became the family motto attached to their coat of arms. In 1362, his son, another Gilbert, built the Pele Tower which can still be seen among what remains of Workington Hall.

Come the seventeenth century the family became ultra-royalist, supporting not only Charles I, but also the Catholic James II. Henry Curwen followed James into exile in France and later was briefly imprisoned in Carlisle Castle for his part in the 1715 Jacobite uprising. But it is in the eighteenth century that we see the Curwen family beginning to transform the town.

Coal had been mined in the area for centuries, even by the Celts whose stone and flint axe heads have been found in some of the older workings where the seams came so close to the surface that they could

Workington Hall

simply be tunnelled into, but it was Henry Curwen (1728-1778) who really opened up the field and made a commercial success of it. He sank as many as fourteen shafts and built the first quay at Harrington, so he could have his share in the profitable export trade with Ireland: Ireland having no fuel supply of its own apart from peat.

By far the most interesting Curwen, however, was not in fact a full blood member of the family. He was born John Christian at Ewanrigg Hall, but in 1782 he married Isabella, his first cousin and Henry's sole surviving heir, and then, not surprisingly, took the family name, becoming John Christian Curwen. Isabella's father had been dead for two years. She was only seventeen and a very considerable heiress indeed, and while it would be silly to think that the money had not entered into his marriage plans, it does seem to have been a love match too, and the townspeople certainly approved of it. They rang the church bells, and the ships in the harbour flew all their flags and fired off their guns. John Christian bought the island of Long Holme on Windermere and renamed it *Bella Isle* (we know it now as *Belle Isle*) and when he extended Harrington harbour that too was known for a while as *Bellaport*. A romantic as well as a very practical and successful businessman — what wife could ask for more?

He was a Member of Parliament for 38 years, first for Carlisle and then for Cumberland and though his party, the Whigs, were in opposition during most of that time, he took his role very seriously. He campaigned passionately in support of the Poor Laws, and did so with dramatic effect, entering the House of Commons on one occasion wearing clogs and a coarse woollen suit to show his colleagues how his constituents lived. Even more dramatically he had a barley loaf, called a "brown Geordie" under one arm and a hard Whillimor Cheese under the other and when he then produced a knife and started sawing away at the crust it is said to have sounded like "the crunching of cinders". I very much doubt if the Speaker would allow anything quite as histrionic as that today, but it does tell us a lot about Curwen. He always put his whole heart into anything he believed in.

It is not only the vitality but the versatility of the man that is so striking. As well as being an active Member of Parliament and a mine owner, he was also an agriculturalist, running a farm a few miles out of town at Schoose. And he wasn't just a *gentleman farmer*, playing at it, as some were in his day. Schoose was an experimental farm of the first importance. He experimented with various types of barley, wheat and turnips and carefully recorded and compared the results. He varied the feedstuffs given to his cattle, calculated the milk yield and the gains and losses in weight, and so that others could benefit from all this he founded the Workington Agricultural Society where he could share his results. Britain was at war and his aim was to try to make the country more self-sufficient. As he once said of his farm, "It has employed hundreds and fed thousands." What foodstuffs he could not supply, he bought wholesale and sold cheaply to his own work people. He was an enlightened employer in so many ways. He even encouraged the formation of Friendly Societies and introduced insurance schemes among his workers, contributing generously to them out of his own pocket.

In the town itself, his greatest achievement was his transformation of Workington Hall, adding the most splendid of extensions to it and overseeing a complete refurbishment. Over the years the Curwen family home had progressed from being a simple medieval dwelling of timber and thatch, to a Pele Tower, and then to an elegant Tudor mansion. Just how elegant we can see from a description written in 1671 by Thomas Denton, "I do not know any one seat in all Britain so commodiously situated for beauty, plenty and pleasure as this is…with large gardens, orchards and long walks, shaded with fir trees on the south, and with all sorts of good fruit, herbs, plants etc.." But John Christian Curwen now had the money to take things even further. He commissioned landscape gardeners and employed John Carr of York, one of the finest provincial architects of the day, to transform it into a magnificent Georgian mansion. It was now to have a library decorated in mahogany and marble, a salon with luxuries of all kinds, a dining room furnished throughout by Gillows of Lancaster and with portraits — one of Isabella of course — by Romney. And outside there was to be a walled kitchen garden with a greenhouse to grow the pineapples which had become all the rage.

Eighteenth century England had led the way in the design of outstandingly beautiful landscaped gardens and the creation of some magnificent neo-classical buildings such as Longleat and Stourhead. It does sound an odd thing to claim today, but if the Hall was still today what it was then, the town would have one of the chief tourist attractions in the north of England. But it hasn't, and we will have to come back to that.

All this building and buying demanded money and there was still enough coal underground to provide it. One seam, simply called the *Great Coal* was ten feet thick in itself and Curwen was said to be exporting around a hundred thousand tons a year. The only problem he faced was that there were not always enough locals to mine it; West Cumberland has never been a populous area, and so John Christian brought over men from Ireland. Five hundred of them. Migrant workers. Now it does not need the brightest of imaginations to guess what happened next. It is all too familiar. They were foreigners. There were too many of them. They all lived together. They spoke a language people couldn't understand. They were taking *our* jobs. And to cap it all, they followed a different religion. They were Roman Catholics. Trouble was not long in starting.

Easter 1814 began with a number of brawls and fights outside the pubs, but it was nothing untoward. Such things happened. On the Sunday though during a scuffle in Elizabeth Street between John Murphy, an Irish tailor, and four local youths he is said to have fired a gun at them. None of then was hurt apparently, but shortly afterwards Murphy was found dead in the street. He had been hit over the head with an axe. No one was arrested.

It would not have taken much to set the simmering violence boiling over and an Orangeman, James Grenan, who came across from Ireland, managed to do precisely that. There were speeches denouncing the Catholics. There was a fife and drum parade (it is all so familiar) through the streets. Hundreds turned out and all too soon it had become a riot. John Christian himself tried to calm matters, but it was past cure. They went from one Irish house to another ransacking as they went. The Catholic church was smashed and desecrated. Many of the Irish fled, but many stayed on to fight. The riots went on for three days until a detachment of the 3rd Kings Own Dragoons had to be called in to restore a semblance of order and it can only have been a semblance as it was another nine months before it was thought safe to let them leave.

You would have thought that working in the mines was dangerous enough in itself without the miners fighting amongst themselves. Even in the early years of the eighteenth century men were working at depths of over 200 feet. Ventilation was poor and the only light they had was from candles, which meant that explosions were almost a commonplace. That or asphyxiation, for as one report tells us "(those) found close to the actual explosion are roasted, or at least burned; others through a sudden loss of air are invariably choked."

Boom years do not last for ever though. By 1820 John Christian was in debt. Costs had been rising and production falling. Pits had to be closed. We would call it *rationalisation* today. It became so bad that by 1824 only one pit, the Isabella, was in full-time production. Still the situation grew worse but in 1836 it was decided to re-open the Lady Pit. John Christian's eldest son, Henry, had taken over by this time, but his interests seem to have been literary more than industrial. The men began to follow a seam which led out under the Irish Sea. They dug for over two miles and even when the seam began to rise they carried on digging until they were less than 80 feet below the sea bed and of that 80 feet little more than 20 was solid rock. What happened was inevitable. At a quarter to nine on the evening of Friday 28th July 1837 the roof collapsed and the sea came flooding in. Of the 57 men and boys working down there at the time, 30 miraculously managed to escape, but 27 were drowned. That was not the only consequence of course: the remainder of the town's mining work force found itself instantly unemployed. A lynch mob went after the manager, Ralph Coxon, but they didn't find him.

In the years that followed, the industry did have its good years, but most of them were bad. Exporting to Ireland was not as profitable as it had been and the new railways were able to bring cheaper Scottish coal into the area. In 1875 a crisis point was reached and the mine owners decided, in their wisdom, that the only way out of the difficult situation they were in was to reduce the men's wages by 15%. A strike was surely predictable, but perhaps that was what they wanted. It lasted for fourteen weeks and when it was over the rate was still cut by 10%. The end was coming and later that year when the Annie Pit closed down, coalmining in Workington was as good as over. It was almost a hundred years before The United Steel Companies sank another shaft near what is now the Ellis Sports Ground, but that closed down too in 1973 and now all that remains of a great industry are the two chimneys and the engine house of Jane Pit which have been preserved and protected as historical monuments.

The story of the iron and steel industry would read very much the same. Over two hundred years of history stand behind it. Brave men and brilliant men. Fortunes made and fortunes lost. Nationalisation and closure.

It was as far back as 1763 when the first, the Seaton Iron Works, opened at Barepot on the north bank of the Derwent and in those days, as well as making wheels and pistons and so on for the shipbuilders and the collieries, they also made iron frying pans and kettle and stoves for the people of the town. Steel was mostly confined to cutlery and small tools as it was very costly to make until Henry Bessemer (1813-1898) came up with a process which can be said to have created a new industry. It was at the *Workington Haematite Iron Company* in 1855 that he made what looks like a simple discovery: that blowing a blast of air through molten pig iron oxidises away all the natural impurities in it, but it was from that moment that large-scale steel making became possible. It could now be used for the structural supports of bridges and it could be used in the making of ships. It was a discovery which changed everything.

It is hard today to know how to react to the closure of such a great industry. Without the men who founded and developed it, our world would not exist. Once we were totally dependent on wood and stone for structure and support. These men gave us the girders that make today's buildings possible. They made it possible to build cars and planes, mobile phones and ipods. yet it is hard in some ways not to feel glad that it is all over and done with. As William Palmer wrote in 1941 in his book *The Verge of Western Lakeland,* "On the Workington shore and the estuary of the Derwent iron and steel works extend for miles" and looking at the old aerial photographs they look like scenes from hell, and at floor level it is even worse. The squalor in which people worked, and not that long ago, is beyond belief. Oh, they look happy enough. They are smiling. But then they are having their photographs taken and that is what you were expected to do. You watched the birdie and you smiled. Richard L. M. Byers, in his book *Workington Iron and Steel* includes a photograph of a 'teemer' manually controlling the flow of molten steel into an ingot less than a yard away from his feet. Clearly he is not tall enough or not at the right height to do it properly, so he is balancing on the rim of an empty mould, a rim which is far narrower than the sole of his boot. He has nothing on his hands, nothing to protect his eyes, and on his head he has a cloth cap. In the minds of the men who owned and managed these works the words *health and safety* might have been Sanskrit or Greek. It is hard to imagine conditions more dangerous, even in the mines. Workers were easily come by and all too often held to be of little account, which is why, I suppose, they were called *hands.*

And after work, what did they come home to? In a report written by the town's Medical Officer of Health, it is stated that in some nine-room houses, such as one in Derwent Street, there were as many as seven families living, most having just one room to live and sleep in, and that to get to the water closet, you could not call it a toilet, they all had to troop through a room that was 'home' to a man, his wife and their three children.

At the same time, up on the hill and away from the grime, there were houses of some elegance and they can still be seen in the area where Park End Road joins Ramsay Brow. Park End, the house which is now the Helena Thompson Museum, is a fine example of domestic Georgian architecture. It was built in 1730 to house the stewards of the Curwen family estates, the earliest of whom were in fact Thompsons, but Helena who had lived in the house for nearly sixty years bought the house from the family in 1934. She was what is known as a benefactor. She built a "shelter for aged men" in Vulcan Park, provided £500 for a new maternity ward and when she died in 1939 she left the house to the council as a museum for the town and district.

Again, it's not much of a museum, to be honest. Downstairs there is a collection of nineteenth century woman's dresses and a re-creation of a tiny Victorian sitting room. Upstairs there are some display boards and photographs and bits and bobs. Among the bits and bobs though I did notice some of the special footballs which have been used during the annual Easter skirmishes between *The Uppies* and *The Downies*. It seems to be not so much a football match but more along the lines of those medieval riots during which one side tries to get the ball from one side of town to the other while stopping the other side who are trying to do the same thing but in the opposite direction. Apart from deliberate murder, that is probably the full extent of the rules.

What did hold my attention upstairs was the model of Workington Hall. In its day it must have been so impressive and up until the 1920's it seems that it was all still intact. Old photographs show us the billiards room, a sumptuous library and the dining room with its Corinthian columns, its marble fireplace and long, gleaming table with its twelve "Hepplewhite-style" chairs, which were later to grace the State Dining Room of the American Embassy in Vienna. But sadly it was around that time that the family began to run out of money and they could simply no longer afford to pay for the repairs which were increasingly needed. The Hall stood empty for long periods of time and must have been getting damper and mustier. The family, not surprisingly, preferred to live in Carlisle or on Belle Island. Mrs Chance-Curwen, the then Lady of the Manor, let it be known that she would happily sell the Hall to the Council, but nothing came of that scheme and in 1939 it was requisitioned by the War Office and turned into a military transit camp. It is not difficult to envisage the devastation – just think of the hob-nailed boots. And sometime during those war years a fire gutted the dining room, damaged the rooms above it and even some of the roof timbers. When the War was over Mrs Chance-Curwen decided to *give* the building to the Council, possibly to escape death duties, and in the hope that it might be converted

Portland Square

into the Town Hall. Perhaps it was unwise of the Council to accept what was now a vandalised, dilapidated ghost of a thing with dry rot everywhere. They could not afford even basic maintenance and before long the lead was being stripped from the roof, lead pipes and guttering were carted off and it was all beyond repair.

But even as a ruin, something could have been preserved. There was a time when the grounds were open to the public; there were guided tours and open-air theatre. Now although you can go into the ground, the building itself is all boarded up, and is a very sad sight. There must have been a point at which someone could have done something to save and preserve what was once a fine building. Now, although there is a plan to rebuild it, the cost will run to close on ten million pounds and it is hard to see how it can be commercially viable, even if, as is hoped, it included units for small businesses and apartments. I cannot see Workington becoming a centre for tourism.

One of the problems with Workington is that it does not seem to have a centre, or possibly it has three centres. The oldest is, or rather was, not far from the Hall and is where Curwen Street and Jane Street meet. It is a tiny square called Market Place, so tiny it gives you a very good idea of just how small medieval and seventeenth century towns were. And yet small as it is, a picture in the Helena Thompson Museum shows it as being called the *Butter Market* and there is a sort of slate umbrella or mushroom in the middle of it to give some protection from the weather to the girls who were selling butter and eggs there. And not far away again is the old covered market hall, but that is closed and derelict now. The narrow roads in this area with names like Curwen Street, Christian Street, Elizabeth Street not only preserve the town's history in their names, they have preserved a feeling of being a small town in themselves. They have kept themselves to themselves and every now and then you can come across a house of quite starling elegance, one particularly caught my eye in Christian Street.

And then there is Portland Square, fully cobbled and so wonderfully picturesque even when the trees aren't in flower. It is just such a pity that it has been allowed to become a car park. The Assembly Rooms in the south west corner were once host to no less a performer than Oscar Wilde. He gave a lecture there in February 1884 entitled *Personal Reminiscences of a Tour of America*. He had not written any of his plays by this time of course, but nor had he caused any scandal.

I met the owner of the house in the opposite corner to the Assembly Rooms and he told me that when he bought it one of the older inhabitants of the Square referred to it as *The Captain's House* and said that there was a story that Fletcher Christian had lived there. These stories of him having got back to England do persist. Interestingly, as he pointed out, there are two round, porthole-like windows in the gable end from which, when the house was built in 1760, there would have been a good view right down to the harbour. At one time the Square even had three inns: The Wheatsheaf, The Coach and Horses and The Green Dragon. The Green Dragon, a posting inn with a history going back centuries, is still there, but is now called The Portland. No sense of history and no imagination. And that's not the only time such a thought crossed my mind in Workington.

In the centre of the Square is a tall grey marble obelisk erected to the memory of Doctor Anthony Peat who died in 1877 and who, as the inscription says, "during a life spent in incessant toil for the relief of human suffering won the love and esteem of all classes." And that must have been true, as it is reported that some three thousand mourners followed his funeral procession and the townsfolk raised £535 for his memorial.

Crossing Washington Street and turning into Pow Street you come across another town centre, this time very much a shopping centre which leads into Finkle Street. Now that is an odd sort of name and I knew there was a Finkle Street in Kendal too and I was pretty sure I had seen one in Carlisle, so when I got home I asked Google about it and learned that there are as many as thirty-two Finkle Streets in England, the furthest south, if you can call it south, being in Boston, Lincolnshire. All the rest are in the north and in what were mostly Viking strongholds. Etymologists say it is derived from an Old Norse word meaning *an angle* and that it denotes a street with a kink in it. But thousands of streets in the north of England must have kinks in them (far more than thirty-two certainly) and some Finkle Streets are very straight. But I also learned that in Cottingham, whose Finkle Street does run dead straight, there is a local tradition that it means a road leading to a market, which many a Finkle Street seems to do, and I think that must be where the name comes from.

Workington's Finkle Street is near a market and also near what is called a *Regeneration Area* where even more shops are being built. At the start of 2006 there was a massive hole in the ground and it did not seem to be meeting with total approval of the locals. A paper seller said to me, and I hadn't raised the subject with him, "Man, they're turning this town into a heap of shite." And only moments later, when I was looking at my street map, a lady passing by said, "You can put that away, pet. It's all out of date. Anything with any character has been pulled down and replaced by a monstrosity."

There is a pub in Workington — actually it is an ex-cinema — called the *Henry Bessemer*, but apart from that the town seems to show very little interest in its past. The harbour is a case in point. In the hundred years before 1860 three hundred ships were built and launched there. It is far larger than the harbour at Maryport, yet whereas in Maryport things are happening, and there is activity and vitality and (I'd go so far as to say) a real sense of beauty, here there is nothing. A vast expanse of dead water. A few people may be walking their dogs and there are a couple of dozen dirty little craft, few of which I would want to trust my life to. It looks to have been cleaned up and that's all that can be said for it. There is not so much as a plaque to record some of the events which happened here: for instance the arrival of Mary Queen of Scots after the defeat of her army at Longside in 1568. She had fled south in disguise to Dundrennan Abbey near Kirkcudbright, hired a fishing vessel and crossed the Solway to land at Workington. Wordsworth wrote one of his more dreadful sonnets about the event, recording how she landed:

> With step preclusive to a long array
> Of woes and degradation hand in hand.

Clearly she felt she could rely on Sir Henry Curwen and he was there to welcome her and to give her refuge in the Hall, for which she presented him with a small agate cup — possibly a travelling chalice — later to be known as *The Luck of Workington* when she left. But her luck had run out and her move to Carlisle Castle was the beginning of an imprisonment which ended with her execution at Fotheringhay.

An even more important visitor, to my way of thinking, was Saint Cuthbert, even though he was dead at the time. The Vikings had invaded the Monastery at Lindisfarne in 793 and they kept coming back, plundering Monkwearmouth and Jarrow and burning down Hexham. In 875, fearing yet another invasion the monks of Lindisfarne took up Cuthbert's wooden coffin — the one you can still see in Durham Cathedral, the one with those wonderful carvings on the side — and they put it on a cart and set off on a long and tortuous journey, hoping they might reach safety in Ireland. But when they reached the Cumberland coast and boarded a ship, a terrible storm broke. They took this to be an omen and a warning that Cuthbert's body was to remain in England, yet even before they had a chance to disembark the ship gave a lurch and the great Lindisfarne Gospels went over the side and looked to be lost for ever. And all this happened at Workington or Derwentmouth as the old story calls it. But, that night, Cuthbert appeared to one of the monks in a dream and told him that the Gospels would be found washed up on the sands at Whithorn in Galloway. And so they were. Well, you don't have to believe it.

Perhaps the one good thing that can be said for the harbour is that when you turn round and head back towards the town you do get a good view of St. Michael's Church. In all probability a church has stood on this site from as early as the 7th Century. Then it would have been seen to be standing on a promontory close to, and possibly almost surrounded by what we know to have been the previous course of the River Derwent, and hence on a site of some strategic importance. Its dedication to St. Michael, the guardian angel, might not have been without significance either. Discoveries of various Viking artefacts and carved stones tend to support this idea, but the first church for which there is clear documentary evidence was built in Norman times, around 1125, when Ketel, Baron of Kendal and founder of the Curwen family, granted the church to St Mary's York, and the Norman tower suggests that like many Border churches, it also afforded protection against invaders. The font, which is in the Baptistry, under the tower, and was discovered in the churchyard in the 1930's dates from just that period. It is said to show the six days of creation, the Sabbath and the Day of Resurrection, but I could not make out anything at all.

Over the years, as the population outgrew the church, the interior was changed repeatedly, with as many as five galleries being added, but by the eighteenth century the town had grown so much that an entirely new church was needed and plans were drawn up that would involve the demolition of all but the old tower. There followed twenty years of legal wrangling between the Curwens and the Lowthers, largely over pews and precedence, but in 1772 the new building was complete, and the tower had been strengthened to take a peel of six bells. If this Georgian building was in any way comparable with St. James's in Whitehaven then sadly the town suffered a real loss in 1887 when fire gutted the interior. Curiously, a local newspaper report makes it sound more exciting than sad. "...thousands of spectators had assembled in the vicinity of the church and the scene, although terrible, was magnificent. Forked flames issued from the windows, the galleries fell, the stone windows toppled over, the roof collapsed and gigantic sheets of flame towered upwards, lighting up the whole of the surrounding neighbourhood for a great distance... The pulpit was seen standing after almost everything else was consumed, the spiral wreaths and showers of sparks which shot upwards from it making a peculiarly picturesque display which will long remain in the memory of those who were near enough to witness it." The reporter seems to have enjoyed the whole thing.

And so another rebuilding, this time in Victorian Gothic with all the inevitable battlements, but 1938 did see some welcome brightening up when the timbers over the chancel were painted red, blue and gold as in Carlisle Cathedral. Then in 1994 there was another fire and the church was reduced to a ruinous shell yet again. But was it sad this time? I find it hard to think so, as the interior of St. Michael's is now one of the most beautiful small churches I have ever been into. It is so full of light and even the colour scheme has been thought out and designed so that your eyes are lifted from the earth colour of the carpet to the blue of the ceiling and its gold stars of the heavens, and as we look up we are surrounded, as the guide says, by a "cloud of witness": a frieze of angels and representations of those great saints who fostered Christianity in the north of England. I warmed to them instantly. These are *our* saints: Ninian, Aidan, Herbert, Kentigern and Bridget on the north gallery and Bega, Oswald, Cuthbert and Wilfred on the south. They are two-dimensional figures with a frank simplicity to them, as though they had been cut from the margins of some illuminated manuscript and in this they provide such a contrast to the figure of St. Michael which we see when we turn back from the altar. This is decidedly not the archangel as we are used to seeing him. There is none of that static superiority he usually wears along with his silver armour. There is a dynamic and living actuality to him as he comes flying down from the west wall on wings of glass, his spear outstretched, to protect us. It is magnificent. It is awesome.

And all this is the work of Edmund Blood. Born in Hartlepool in 1946, Edmund Blood studied Fine Art at St Martin's and Camberwell Colleges of Art in London, where he met his wife Mary, a graphic designer. In 1973 they moved to Cumbria, where Edmund taught first in Workington and then as Head of Art at The Lakes School in Windermere. He was a good teacher and a successful one, but began to find that the demands of the job made it difficult for him to give his own painting the time and dedication he wanted to, so in 1996, encouraged by John Parkinson of the Upfront Gallery near Hutton in the Forest, Penrith, who offered him an exhibition of his paintings, he took early retirement and then, as he told an interviewer, he had "… the space to daydream, when the mind wanders and you look at things with an intensity and a depth." Happily, this new "space" coincided with the refurbishment of St Michael's, and he was commissioned to design the frieze of "frosted glass" windows and the plaques of the Northern Saints. Working in his studio in Middlegate House in Great Clifton, a wonderful and rambling house which dates back to 1774, he finished the figures in an astonishingly short space of time. And it does seem so fitting that a man who had so loved drawing and painting pictures of buildings should have been given this opportunity to help turn a burned-out ruin into such a thing of beauty.

Edmund was not a religious man in the accepted sense, but he did, as his wife Mary told me, have a great love of the language of the King James Bible and the Book of Common Prayer and he must have had a deep spiritual awareness, otherwise he would not have walked the whole of the 500 mile Medieval Pilgrim Route to Santiago de Compostela which he did in 1999. Having walked it myself, I know that you are never quite the same again after that. Holiness, even piety, is evident in is work, but there is not a trace of sentimentality.

The work is very much of our time. The frieze is not "frosted glass". It looks to have been etched, but is in fact a thin layer of sign-maker's plastic, cut by computer and fixed onto the glass. And the saints, although they may look to have stepped out of a medieval manuscript, are made of a succession of layers of shaped fibre laminates. The archangel's body is also MDF board and the complex shapes which go together to make his wings were cut by a new process which uses a water-jet. It is 21st century work, and work which will last. There might have been so much more of Edmund's work for us to see, but sadly he died of a heart attack in 2002, little more than a year after the service of dedication. At his memorial service John Parkinson read from Edmund's notebooks. One extract I like reads: " 'Art is illusion', someone said; they were wrong. Life is the illusion — art is real. On a blank sheet of paper, with the simplest of materials, you can create order, meaning and emotion … making order out of chaos, telling it like it is, like it was, and, above all, like it should be."

There is another fine piece of work in St Michael's and that is the 15th Century tomb of Sir Christopher Curwen and his wife Elizabeth. The fire reduced it to a heap of rubble in 1994, but has been so perfectly restored by Seamus Hannah of York that you would never know.

One of the features of old churches that always catches my eye is the list of rectors. It takes so very few names to reach back into the distant past. If you could bring them all back to life they would only fill the front pews. In St Michael's there are 45 names, beginning in 1150 with someone simply called Walter. And then there is one called John Wordsworth, William's eldest son, who was here from 1834-1837.

I could not possibly end this chapter, however, without recording that there was one other great man who once lived here, even if only briefly, and that was Bill Shankly, who managed Workington Reds from January 1954 to December 1955, before going on to Huddersfield and then to Anfield and Liverpool's glory days, and those glorious one-liners of his. Such as this, said on the training ground to that most fearsome of defenders, Tommy Smith: "Get that poof bandage off. What do you mean you've hurt your knee? That's not your knee. That's Liverpool's knee."

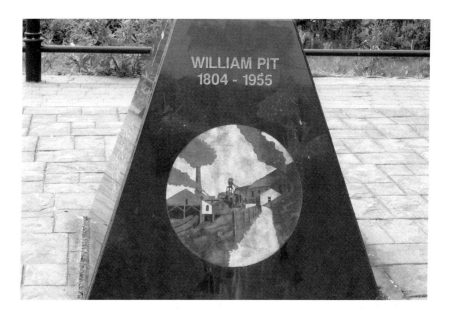

Five:

Harrington. Parton. Moresby Hall. Rum Butter. Smuggling. U-Boat attack. Whitehaven. The Lowther family: 'Farthing Jimmy' & 'Wicked Jimmy'. WhitehavenDevelopment Committee. The Beacon. John Paul Jones. Wellington Pit Disaster. Jonathan Swift. The Harbour. Explosion at William Pit. Richard Ayton. St Nicholas Church – another fire. John Gale & George Washington. The Rum Story. Haig Mining Museum. Corkickle. Whitehaven Rugby League.

Like so many of the other towns up and down this coast, Harrington began as a few small cottages gathered together at the water's edge and

Above: The William Pit Memorial

its history has followed a pattern so familiar that there's really no need to rehearse it again: coal was mined, a harbour built, its iron and steel industry flourished a while, then failed. What does give it some slight difference is that there is now hardly a trace of its industrial past to be seen and certainly not as you go through on the train. It is as though it has drifted sleepily back to its early days again. I remember thinking when I first saw it that if it was in the south of England, or in Italy, or anywhere else, its compact little harbour would be full to capacity with the poshest of sleek boats and property prices would be beyond belief, let alone the pockets of the people who live there now. I have to say though that getting off the train and seeing the rest of Harrington at first hand soon punctured that fantasy.

A few miles further on comes Parton, a different case altogether, perhaps because it has never had a harbour. There were some attempts to have one built. The Fletcher family of Moresby Hall tried, but they were small fry compared with the Lowthers, who forcibly opposed them and so it seems doubly unfair now that the pub in the Square should be called the *Lowther Arms*. They seem to have won every round. All the Fletchers ever managed was a pier and that was destroyed in a storm. Their family home, Moresby Hall is a Grade One Listed Building and it is claimed that Inigo Jones was involved in the re-modelling of its front façade. He may well have been, but it still looks weird to me, as though it has been put together out of grey Lego. It is so weird-looking that it doesn't surprise me one whit that builders should have found some skeletons under the fireplace in the entrance hall. I'd have been more surprised if they hadn't.

Across the road, on the site of an extensive Roman Fort, stands another inexcusably dour nineteenth century church, dedicated to St Bridget, and alongside that is the arch of the medieval church which it replaced. Why this arch was preserved and how it is that it is still standing, I do not know. But we do know that John Wordsworth was rector there from 1829 until he went to Workington and that his father stayed with him and his spoiled-little-rich-girl wife, Isabella Curwen, who seems, as they say, to have enjoyed ill health. Very wisely, father Wordsworth must have decided to go out on some long walks while he was with them, as he managed to write three of his *Evening Voluntaries* while he was there in 1823.

Look round; — of all the clouds not one is moving;
'Tis the still hour of thinking, feeling, loving,
Silent, and steadfast as the vaulted sky,
The boundless plain of waters seems to lie —

Going back to Parton, there is a delightful though improbable (how well those two words go together) story of Cumberland Rum Butter having had its origin there. It is claimed that a group of smugglers, pursued by the Excise men, hid out in a cave, but the hunt went on and on and they had to stay there for several days and as all they had to eat was the contraband they had been smuggling into the country they had do something with that, and it just so happened that it was rum, butter and sugar, and so that is how… Yes, well.

There is a tendency, I think, to romanticise smuggling. It may stem in part from Kipling's poem, *A Smuggler's Song*, which once upon a time everybody knew.

Five and twenty ponies
Trotting through the dark —
Brandy for the Parson,
'Baccy for the Clerk.
Laces for a lady, letters for a spy,

And watch the wall, my darling, when the Gentlemen go by!

But they were by no means all *Gentlemen*. They were involved in what today we would call *organised crime* and people killed and were killed in the process of it. Quite simply, there was money in it and particularly in the 'trade' with the Isle of Man, or that 'Warehouse of Frauds' as the Revenue Men used to call it. Henry IV had granted the island to Sir John Stanley and his heirs and in 1670 the then 'Lord of Man' had the bright idea that if he were to make a drastic reduction in the duty to be paid on imported goods it might just possibly encourage some of England's wealthier merchants to settle and set up in business there. And of course he was right. It was off-shore trading, the Jersey of its day. Very soon brandy was selling on the Isle of Man for half the price that it fetched on the mainland. One boat alone, intercepted off Whitehaven, was found to be carrying 200 gallons of brandy and 20 gallons of Canary Wine. This was very big business, run by very serious men, and when their goods were taken from them and impounded, armed gangs could be counted on to fight to get them back. Rum butter may or may not have been one of their claims to fame, but I am sure they had many other claims to infamy.

There is one other curious story featuring Parton, but it looks to be due less to someone's fertile imagination than to Chinese whispers. There is a website report that the village was hit by a torpedo from a German submarine during World War II, but that the only casualty was a dog. Silly old Germans. The troubling thing about this story is that the Germans weren't silly, were they? And why would anyone fire a torpedo into a shallow bay that didn't even have a harbour? A local historian tells a quite different story. And a very factual one. A German submarine U-24 sailed into Parton Bay at 4.40 in the morning on 16th August 1915 (So it was World War I!) to shell the previously *German-owned* chemical works up on the hill at Lowca. So they knew exactly what they were doing. And for good measure they then fired off a few rounds at Whitehaven before heading out to sea again. The one place that was not fired on was Parton and there is no report of any dog being hurt, but apparently there were some delays to the train service that morning. And that appears to be the truth of it. Not a lot doesn't happen in Parton seemingly and while it can boast some fine eighteenth century houses, that same railway line, from the moment it was built, high up on its embankment, totally blocked out any view the villagers' had of the sea.

But let's forget about Parton and all the other boring bits of the coast along there and get ourselves down to Whitehaven. After Maryport and Workington, the two ugly sisters (well, if not exactly ugly, certainly pulchritudinously challenged) Whitehaven is a veritable Cinderella. In this version of the story, however, Cinders not only made her wishes, but, sensible northern girl that she was, she seems to have remembered to get herself home well before twelve o'clock and so has got to keep the lot.

Going back to its beginnings, Whitehaven can be said to have been made by the Lowther family. And what a family. Just reading their history can be dizzying – so many James and Johns flickering past like figures on a roundabout. They were almost certainly of Norman origin and their family tree can be traced back to the late twelfth century, which makes them one of the oldest families on record in England. Sir Hugh de Lowther was Attorney General to Edward I and was the first of the family to be knighted, but the family's fortunes began properly with Sir John

Whitehaven Harbour.

Lowther (1582-1637) who firmly believed that making money was what really counted in this world and he passed this belief down to his descendants. Under his grandson, another Sir John (1642-1706) Whitehaven grew from a small village to a town of close on 3000 people. It was he who expanded the coalmines, who developed ship building and all those other industries allied to it, the sail makers, the blacksmiths, the painters, rope makers and so on, and it was he who began the tobacco trade with Virginia. The estate then passed to his son, Sir James, who at his death in 1755 had become the richest commoner in the country with a fortune estimated to be in excess of £50 million in today's terms, but was such a miser that he was always known as "Farthing Jimmy". Under his management coal production increased and imports of tobacco reached twelve million pounds in weight a year, making Whitehaven the second most important port after London.

He was followed by another Sir James, this one being known as "Wicked Jimmy". Whereas in the days of the previous Sir James, the town had seen the building of the Cupola and St. James's and Holy Trinity Church, "Wicked Jimmy" oversaw the growth of the slums — hundreds of back-to-back terraces on Mount Pleasant with no water supply or sewerage. It was housing fit only for animals. The poor died of cholera in their hundreds. One incident alone shows the nature of the man. It was in 1791. There was considerable subsidence over one of his pits and he was sued for damages. Rather than accept responsibility and pay up, Wicked Jimmy's response was to close down all his pits, despite the suffering caused to the workforce, and to keep them closed until he was guaranteed indemnity against any future such claims.

As a Member of Parliament he was equally unscrupulous, controlling nine seats in Parliament. They were known as "Jimmy's Ninepins" and he was quite prepared to force the members out if they didn't do and vote *exactly* how he told them.

"William the Good" who succeeded him certainly did some good to the Wordsworth family. The poet's father had been steward to the Lowther family estates, but was, it seems, very rarely paid and it was this William Lowther who settled the debt which had then been outstanding for some twenty years.

In the nineteenth century the fifth earl was more keen on sporting affairs than business, and was remembered for two remarkable things: winning a bet that he could walk a hundred miles in twenty-four hours and setting up a fund for boxing's Lonsdale Belts. It was death duties which eventually forced the seventh earl to sell off all his Whitehaven estates.

I think one of the biggest debts Whitehaven owes to the Lowther family is to whichever of them it was who, with some assistance from Sir Christopher Wren, decided on the grid-iron design for its street system. It has given the town such a distinctive, open, uncluttered look — long straight vistas, coupled with those sudden surprises as when you are walking along Lowther street and glance up and see the full face of St. James's Church. It was said by Pevsner to have the "finest Georgian church interior in the county", and certainly its Wedgwood-like ceiling not only lifts up your eyes, it lifts the spirit too.

But while Whitehaven certainly owes a lot to its past, the changes which have been brought about in recent years are, in their way, perhaps even more of an achievement. A few simple facts. In 2002 the *Sunday Times* listed Whitehaven among the country's top ten seaside towns. It was named the Best Town Centre in the UK in the British Council's Shopping Centres Environment Award in 2001, beating off competition from twenty other entries. Its flower displays have won it the Cumbria in Bloom title more times than any other town in the county and it has come close to winning the Britain in Bloom award.

How did all this come about? By the early seventies, the town and particularly the harbour area was looking very sad, little better than Maryport or Workington, and it was then that BNFL began repair and restoration work on the fabric of some of the older buildings. Perhaps it was in the hope of attracting a new and more qualified workforce. At first progress was slow. In the late 80's a consortium of English Partnerships, BNFL and Cumbria County Council was set up, but it was with the foundation in 1993 of the Whitehaven Development Company, that new schemes sprang into life.

The harbour had gone into bankruptcy the year before, which might have been a blessing as the chief import, phosphate rock brought in by bulk carriers from Morocco, was a dusty, dirty business and the unwanted residue was being dumped into the sea, regardless of the pollution it was causing. The Development Company's first and key decision was that there would be no more imports of that nature and that Whitehaven was instead to be a leisure port. It now has a three hundred berth marina and is the main tourist centre of the west coast.

What the team of four excelled in was fund raising. Money came in from the European Development Fund, The Millennium Commission, the Lottery and many other sources. In the last twelve years they have raised and spent over £60 million, resurfacing the Quays, building new dock gates, the forty metre high tower *The Crows Nest*, and opening exhibition centres such as *The Rum Story* and *The Beacon*.

At first sight *The Beacon* has the look of an old lighthouse, or watch tower, or Customs House, yet it is a new building, purpose-built as an Exhibition Centre. It is best to begin by going up to the top floor where the view takes in the whole of the harbour and most of the town and then as you work your way down there are audio-visual displays, tableaux and recorded voices tracing the history of the varied industries — the ship building, the coal mines, and the tobacco trade for which Whitehaven is famous, as well as those aspects of its past which are rather less creditable — the mining disasters, the terrible slums and the town's involvement with the slave trade. One of *The Beacon's* most important exhibits 'celebrates' this. It is the *Beilby Goblet*, one of the finest examples of early enamelled glass. It was made to commemorate the launching in 1763 of the slave ship the *King George*. On one side is the royal coat of arms of George III and on the other a painting of the ship surmounted by the words "Success to the African Trade of Whitehaven". The Corning Museum of Glass in New York tried to buy it in 1985 but thankfully the Museum managed to raise £59,000 to prevent its export and keep it in Whitehaven.

After seeing everything they have to show you in *The Beacon* it is a good place from which to start a walk around the harbour. A few yards to the left are three small ancient-looking cannons. They do *look* ancient and it would spoil it a bit if they weren't, so I haven't asked. The first one has the bronze figure of a ruffian driving his marlin spike into it — spiking it — to render it useless. What is being commemorated here of course are the exploits of Captain John Paul Jones during the American War of Independence. He is credited with having led the last invasion of England, but *invasion* does seem to be something of an overstatement. It all depends which side you are looking at it from. One view, the American view, is that his audacity and daring in bringing the war to the very shores of England struck fear into the heart of our nation and that he is therefore rightly called *The Father of the American Navy* and fully deserved President Roosevelt's decision in 1913 to have his remains re -interred in an elaborate tomb in the Crypt of the Chapel of the United States Navy Academy in Annapolis. Another view makes the whole episode sound more like something out of the Keystone Cops.

He was born John Paul, the son of a gardener, in Arbigland, Kirkcud-bright, in 1747 and at the age of thirteen was apprenticed on board a vessel ironically called the *Friendship* out of Whitehaven. Still only seventeen he was appointed Third Mate on the maiden voyage of the slave ship *King George,* the same vessel commemorated by the *Beilby Goblet* in *The Beacon.* He did the Africa run for several years and must have greatly impressed his superiors as he gained his first command when he was aged twenty-one. It was not long though before he had acquired a reputation for brutality, having had one seaman flogged almost to death, and on another ship, when a mutiny broke out over pay — or rather non-pay — he ran the ringleader through with his sword. He claimed that it had been in self-defence and no charges were brought, but he thought it best to lie low in America for a while and it was then that he took on the name of Jones.

When the War of Independence began he was given a commission in the Congressional Navy and made captain of a privateer *The Ranger.*

Whether he had some personal grudge against Whitehaven because of something that happened to him there as a small boy, or whether he chose it simply because he had a good knowledge of the lay-out of the harbour and its defences, we will never know, but it was there he headed under cover of darkness on the night of 22nd April 1778. Two boats were landed. One headed for the North Harbour and its crew were meant to set fire to the ships there, but it is at this moment that the farce begins. They had been at sea for some time and as soon as they saw Nicholas Allison's public house, *The Red Lion,* in they went and stayed so long drinking that their candles had gone out! Jones's men had successfully overpowered the small garrison and spiked the guns, and they had managed to set fire to a collier, the *Thompson,* but it was raining so hard that it put that fire out. Meanwhile, one of the crew, David Freeman, an Irishman, who only wanted to get off the ship and get back home, slipped out of *The Red Lion,* and went knocking on the doors of the townspeople to warn them what was happening. People came running out of their houses and Jones and his men were lucky to reach their boats and get away. But it all ended happily as in 1998, during Whitehaven's first Maritime Festival, a small detachment of American Marines came to take part and the Harbour Master presented them with a signed Proclamation officially forgiving the United States for what they had done, or what they thought they had done. And it does seem only right and proper now that although *The Red Lion* no longer exists, Whitehaven has a new pub down near the harbour called the *John Paul Jones*, with a brightly-painted sign showing a dashing naval hero.

High up on the cliffs above *The Beacon* is the "Candle Stick Chimney" which is not in fact a chimney at all, but an air vent for the Wellington Pit, its unusual design seemingly based on an actual candlestick which graced the Lowther's mantelpiece. It was the brainchild of the architect Sidney Smirke (1798-1877) whose elder brother, Robert, had built Lowther castle. Sidney has an impressive list of architectural achievements to his credit, including the wonderful circular Reading Room of the British Museum, Burlington House and the Carlton Club, but he seems to have let his imagination run away with itself when he drew up the plans for the Wellington Pit. When he had finished it looked far more like a traditional castle than did Lowther Castle. It had a massive keep, turrets and lofty crenulated walls, as well as the peculiar "Chimney". But the Wellington Pit is better known for being the site of the town's worst pit disaster. It was in May 1910. Over one hundred and forty men had gone down for the evening shift when there was an explosion of such ferocity that rescue teams were driven back time and again by the smoke and the heat. Galleries were blocked off to try to contain the fire that had become an inferno down there, but it was several months before it was finally extinguished and the charred bodies of 136 miners brought to the surface. You would think that such a loss of life might be enough to close down a mine for good, but money takes precedence over life and it went on producing coal for another twenty-two years before it was deemed to be uneconomical.

Not far from the " Candle Stick Chimney" is what the Guide Maps show as *Jonathan Swift's House.* He himself wrote that his nurse was from Whitehaven and that when she heard that a relative of hers living here, whom she thought was going to leave her some money, had been taken ill and was thought likely to die, she upped and off, carrying little baby Jonathan with her. She didn't neglect her job, you see. It was three years apparently before his mother found out where he was and had him taken back to Ireland, but this nurse must have been a very unusual woman, as apart from being an accomplished kidnapper, she had also taught the future satirist to read and write and, so he claimed, by the age of three he could read any chapter of the Bible put in front of him. I was told that it was from looking down on all the tiny figures scurrying about in the harbour that he got the idea for the Lilliputians. Who knows? Perhaps one can imagine the child looking at the little boats and thinking to himself that it would be an easy matter to catch up some dozens of their hawsers in each hand and tow them out of the harbour as he would later have Gulliver do in Blefescu. Who knows?

But if he were to look down on the harbour now, there would be little he would recognise and certainly not at night when the whole area becomes a living sculpture in light. The florescent *Wave* along the Lime Tongue, reflected by the waters of the marina — blue on one side, green on the other — leads the eye to the spectacular *Crow's Nest,* a 40m high structure made to represent a ship's mast. By day it is plain white, but at night computer-controlled lighting, determined by changes in the wind speed, transforms it into all the colours of the rainbow. Even Gulliver met nothing to equal that in all his travels.

The town's history is everywhere, even recorded on the backs of the benches, where there are plaques telling you of the Wellington Pit Disaster, or that in 1415 a member of the Lowther Family fought at the Battle of Agincourt.

The beginnings of the harbour can be dated back to 1634 when Sir Christopher Lowther had the Old Quay built to provide shelter for the little collier vessels sailing to and from Ireland, but later the American trade — the importing of rum and sugar — brought in far larger ships and in 1734 what is known as The Sugar Tongue was built. There used to be a slate-roofed cover over it to give some protection from the weather, something the workers must have been glad of in more recent times when it was largely fish that was being landed. But all that was cleared away together with the ice plant and the fuel bunkers as part of the £16 million Millennium regeneration programme. If the walkway of the Sugar Tongue is white today, it is not from sugar, but bird shit. The gulls have decided that it is the perfect place for them and that includes the tables, which is a shame as they have been well-designed and with a sense of humour – for example one has a pile of coins on it and the words "Money for Old Rope". At the far end of it is another of Whitehaven's statues: this one is of a lad sitting on a capstan with a telescope to his eye and looking out to sea, hoping, it would seem, for the first glimpse of his father's ship on its way home to Whitehaven.

On the next quay, The Lime Tongue, the old bollards are still there, deeply scored and scarred by the tens of thousands of cables and hawsers which must have been tied around them and the strain they had to take as the tides pulled at the vessels. The benches here record all the different trades, imports and exports which once kept it so busy: sugar and coal, tobacco and timber, and, of course, fish. At the end of the Tongue, the Crow's Nest records distance in nautical miles and the bearing of ports from Reykjavik to Tokyo, and of two ports which tell something of the darker side of the town's history: the Ivory Coast 2954 miles away on a bearing of 180 °, and Antigua 3476 miles, bearing 230°. Whatever you think of the trade you have to admire the daring of the men who covered such vast distances and under sail.

"Boy on capstan", Whitehaven Harbour

On your right, as you are heading towards the fish dock is the Inland Revenue Office. This is a large sandstone building which looks like an old warehouse they have taken over and converted, whereas in fact it is a very recent building but so designed that it fits in perfectly with the harbour side. It is such a sensible piece of town planning, it is only a pity the same amount of forethought didn't go into the Police Station in Scotch Street, once nominated, so I am told, as the Nastiest Nick in the country. Local legend has it that the architect was commissioned to design two and the plans got swapped, so that somewhere in the south, they say, somewhere like Crawley or Milton Keynes, they have the most delightful Georgian Police Station. It would not surprise me.

Before you get to the fish dock, there are more pieces of art work: Alan Clark's *Whiting Shoal* and then even the dock gates themselves have been designed as a net with a shoal of fish caught in it.

I was watching a trawler being unloaded there once and two things puzzled me: the name *Georg Lou – N* and the language the crew were speaking. I couldn't make it out, even after I heard the skipper call one of the deck hands a *fuckin' eejit*. He was a Scot, no doubt of that, but the rest… they sounded Russian, and when one of the hands came up onto the dockside he told me that they were mostly Latvian. Tom Nicholson, who owned the *Georg Lou-N* and five other boats, explained that local men wouldn't do the job. Too much like hard work; he had to get his men from an agency and the Latvians were good lads. Oh, and *Georgina Louise Nicholson* was his young daughter. He blamed the Irish and the Spaniards for the shortage of fish, but was pleased enough with the eight tonne of scallops – queenies – the trawler had just brought in.

Looking inland from the dock you can see a low, green building which is now the *Cumbrian Steel Stock,* but was once the site of the notorious William Pit. Sunk in 1804, it exploded fourteen times in the 150 years that it was open, killing more than two hundred, and not just men, but women, girls and boys. It was in April 1947 though that the worst explosion of all took place. One hundred and four men lost their lives in an explosion so devastating that it was a week before all the bodies could be recovered. With such a loss of life and so many to be buried the local gravediggers could not cope and Whitehaven miners themselves were called upon to dig the graves of their *marras*. Reading down a list of casualties I counted twelve from the little village of Parton alone, four of them from the same street. The explosion left Parton with ten widows and thirty-two children without a father. But still coal went on being mined from that same pit for another eight years. It was not an industry which had room for sentimentality.

It is nearly impossible for us to have any real understanding of what life must have been like for those who worked down those pits in the early years, but any sentimental feelings of our own we may have take a very severe knock when we read an account by Richard Ayton of a visit he made to Whitehaven's William Pit in 1813. It is reprinted in *"The Most Dangerous Pit in the Kingdom",* a history of the William Pit written by Ray Devlin and Harry Fancy. Ayton's account of all that he saw down there has a stark brutality to it which quite matches the brutality of what he actually saw. He was a first rate reporter and some of the pictures he gives us, we are unlikely to forget. What we have to keep in mind is that he was fundamentally sympathetic to the people working there, yet at the same time he was a realist. The women, for example. "…we were called upon to make way for a horse, which passed by with its long line of baskets and driven by a young girl covered with filth, debased and

Unloading scallops at Whitehaven

profligate and uttering some low obscenity as she hurried by us. We were frequently interrupted in our march by the horses proceeding in this manner with their cargoes to the shaft, and always driven by girls all of the same description, ragged and beastly in their appearance and with a shameless indecency in their behaviour, which awe-struck as one was by the gloom and loneliness around one, had something quite frightful in it and gave the place the character of hell." What shocks him, and us too, is that for all the wretchedness and filth it does not stop these girls getting up to acts of "bestial debauchery" down there in the dark galleries, "without pausing to enquire if it be father and daughter, or brother and sister."

As he says, "The people in the mines are looked upon as mere machinery, of no worth or importance beyond their horse power." He is certainly no sentimentalist, but he ends his account with a long and impassioned plea to end the employment — the slavery he calls it, and not without reason — of women and children in the mines. Children would fight and scream with terror, he tells us, when they were first sent down into that dark, but people are always found "brutal enough to force them to compliance." It went on like this for another thirty years until the First

Coal Mines Act of 1843 when women, and boys under the age of ten, were no longer allowed to be employed underground.

After reading this account it struck me as even odder when I came across a poem written in 1755 by John Dalton (not the chemist, this one was a reverend gentleman) with the title *A Descriptive Poem, Addressed to Two Ladies, at their Return from Viewing The Mines near Whitehaven.* The two ladies in question were daughters of Lord Lowther and the pit must have been the Saltom as the poem makes it clear that they were in galleries which ran under the sea.

> At last the long descent is o'er;
> Above your heads the billows roar.

The Saltom Pit had opened in 1729 and was the first to mine coal from under the Irish Sea. Being Lord Lowther's daughters there is no doubt that they would have been taken good care of, but even so they must have been an intrepid pair of young ladies who would go down into those

> … chambers of the deep,
> Whose jetty pillars seem to groan
> Beneath a ponderous roof of stone.

It is so hard to picture. What on earth — or rather under the earth — did they wear?

There is a Memorial Garden there now marking the site of the William Pit, and recording the list of disasters it suffered over the years, but sadly the plaque has been vandalised and where there were once flowers it is just a mass of weeds. I would have thought someone in the town cared enough to look after it.

There is one beautiful, flower-filled garden in what feels like the centre of the town, and where St Nicholas Church stands, but which isn't a church any longer. Like the parish church in Workington, and now Holm Cultram, this too caught fire. It was in August 1971. It is thought that an electrical fault in the organ sparked a fire in the dust that had been collecting in it over the years and the nave and the sanctuary were totally destroyed. Re-building was considered, but the authorities decided against it. Instead it has become the *St. Nicholas Centre,* with what is obviously a very popular refreshment room and a booth selling souvenirs and postcards. If you ask the lady selling the postcards, she will unlock a little door beside her and let you go up into the tower, climbing one of the narrowest and tightest spiral staircases I have ever encountered, but it is worth it for the view, the wealth of church silver on display up there and a magnificent, ancient clock. It hasn't surrendered all its hold on the faithful though; there is a small chapel separated from the refreshment area by an attractive glass screen with a design symbolising the other two Whitehaven churches which no longer exist: Christ Church and Holy Trinity.

I am told that Whitehaven has in the region of two hundred Grade II listed buildings and time and again as you walk along the streets in the older areas near the harbour you see a plaque commemorating the worthies and the "captains of industry" who once lived there. 25 Roper Street, for example, was the home of the Brocklebank family who founded the world's oldest registered shipping line.

A thousand vessels were built in Whitehaven in the eighteenth and nineteenth centuries, including some of the fastest and most elegant of the famous *Clippers*, but as ships became bigger and bigger it proved to be increasingly difficult, not to say hazardous, launching them in the shallow waters of the Solway and the industry came to an end in 1900.

Generally speaking, ships had always been purpose-built to meet a specific need, but the Brocklebanks were speculators as well as shipwrights and they built to sell, becoming so successful that eventually they outgrew Whitehaven and in 1865 they moved their business to Liverpool where they flourished for more than a century before being taken over by Cunard.

Going down Queen Street, you can't fail to notice No. 152. Even in a town with so many fine buildings, it strikes you as being a perfect example of that elegant, understated grace which is the Georgian town house, plain-fronted, two-storey, sash-windowed, with its ornamental wrought-iron railings and a fanlight under the flat arch. This was once the home of the Gale family, who were among the leading traders with North America, exporting manufactured goods, and shipping back timber and tobacco. Especially tobacco from Virginia. It was the tobacco trade which made Whitehaven the second most important port in the country after London. In the year 1749 alone, twelve million pounds in weight was imported from the Chesapeake Bay area, and that was when there were only forty-seven vessels trading. The number later increased to almost one hundred and fifty.

It was John Gale, an Irish dissenter, who was the first member of the family to decide to live in Whitehaven. That was in the middle of the seventeenth century, and it was he who set up the trade, but it is his grandson, George, who is by far the most interesting member of the family and who is Whitehaven's most important connection with the United States. In 1700, when he was trading in Virginia, he met and married a wealthy widow and brought her and her three children back to England with him. She was already pregnant when she arrived in Whitehaven and seems to have contracted a fever, perhaps on the voyage, and "doubtful of the recovery of my present sickness" as she wrote in her will, she left her "loving husband" the very substantial sum of one thousand pounds, with whatever was left of her assets over and above that to be divided between him and the children. Sadly, she died in January 1701, her African servant also died less than a month later and the new baby survived only another four months. When news of all this reached Virginia, her husband's family successfully contested the will and had the children returned to America where they took their father's name again: the name of *Washington.* And so it was that Augustine, her second son, became in 1732 the father of the first President of the United States. If the argument over the will had gone in George Gale's favour, Augustine would have grown up as a Whitehaven lad — he had already started at Appleby Grammar School — and who knows what the changes to history might have been. Curiously, George Gale himself went back across the Atlantic, remarried, had four sons and founded the town of Whitehaven in Maryland, where he died, whereas the remains of his American wife Matilda were buried in St. Nicholas' Churchyard in Whitehaven in Cumberland. There is no way of knowing exactly where any longer of course, but there is a plaque on the wall to commemorate her.

A few yards away, in Lowther Street, at number 27 is *The Rum Story: The Dark Spirit of Whitehaven.* Earlier on I was rather critical of places which claim to be museums, but which are little more than a collection of old photographs and a few display boards, but this exhibition is absolutely everything which they are not. For a start, it is full, of *things,* and what's more it is housed in and incorporates the original, mid-eighteenth shop, courtyards, cellars and bonded warehouses of the Jefferson family, Whitehaven's premier importers of rum. When you go inside, you are where it all happened.

It was in 1780 that Henry Jefferson of Whitehaven, a master mariner involved in the Virginia tobacco trade, married Ann Tweedie, the daughter of a wealthy plantation owner in Antigua and when they came back to England they set up business here in Lowther Street importing fine wines from Spain and Portugal, and rum, sugar and molasses from the West Indies. And for two hundred years their business flourished. They supplied the popular, if sometimes rather disreputable, Punch Houses of Georgian London and it was the Jefferson Company which supplied wines and spirits to the White Star Shipping Company, so, sadly, it was probably their stock that went down with the *Titanic.* It was competition from supermarkets and chain stores which brought about the Company's closure, but not until 1998. In less than two years though the Whitehaven Development Company, with a grant of £3 million from the Millennium Commission had opened the exhibition as it is today, keeping what was best and most interesting of the old and brilliantly re-creating much, much more so that now it tells the whole of the story.

The Jefferson's office, the first room we see, is very much as it was left and yet it must have been bizarrely antiquated for its time, as the high stools and the desks are positively Dickensian and have far more of the 1890's to them than the 1990's, but if going through that door is a surprise, nothing prepares us for the next: we suddenly find ourselves standing among the towering trees and in the mottled light of the Antiguan rainforest, complete with birdsong. This is what the island would have been like when Columbus 'discovered' it and before the English settlers arrived in the seventeenth century and began to establish the first sugar plantations. Tucked way in a corner of this "rainforest" is a re-creation of a sugar cane factory, hot and squalid and operated of course by African slaves. But before we go any further into that part of the story, we pass into one of the company's bonded vaults, full of bottles (empty ones) covered in the dust and dirt of ages, and with straw on the floor so that you seem to be smelling another century as well as seeing it.

Upstairs we see and hear (thankfully this time we are spared the smell) what conditions were like on the slave ships involved in the "triangular trade", ships capable of carrying as many as seven hundred slaves at a time. We see how they were chained and packed in so close together in the dark. Particularly horrifying — because nothing special is made of them — are the manacles and those spiked neck collars which were used as punishments.

There is then a video of the rum making process as it is carried on today, taking us from the crushing of the raw cane, through the fermentation and distillation to the final product, which in the eighteenth century was so popular in the new Punch Houses in London. And next there is a graphic re-creation of just such a House, based on one of Hogarth's paintings. One 'young lady' is smilingly filling a young toff's glass while another filches his watch. There is so much to see: Rum and the navy; Rum and the Smugglers; and even the story of no-rum — Prohibition in America and the exploits of Eliot Ness and his 'untouchables'. And at the end of it all — at the end of your guided tour — you are given — what else? — a glass of rum! And there has been so much to take in that you need it.

Oh, and I learned the names of the various barrels in descending order of size: hogshead and barrel and kinderkin, firkin and pin. It is almost a 'found poem'.

But don't go rushing out. Before you go back out into Lowther Street, check you watch, as every half hour a crazy, ornamental clock, designed by John Parkinson of Upfront Gallery near Penrith, sets itself off: flags begin to fly, parrots flap their wings, sugar cane sprouts and is chopped down with machetes, wheels and cogs turn round, a boat sails over some very choppy seas — presumably back to Whitehaven and the Jeffersons — and rum flows out, first into rows of copper flagons and then into the waiting barrels. And finally the bottles of rum at the base begin to revolve as they too are filled. They are dated 1775, I noticed, the year before the American Declaration of Independence. It is great fun and well worth waiting for. And if you are too early, there is plenty of good food to be had in the café.

Going back to The Beacon, if you turn left when you come out and head towards the Old Quay you quickly come upon another of Colin Telfer's works and possibly his finest. It is called "The End of an Era" and commemorates the men and women who worked in the coal mines. On one side there are figures representing three different types of worker: a deputy overman, a mines rescue worker and screen lass. The screen lasses were the women who toiled non-stop picking lumps of stone and slate out from the coal as it came up to the surface. This sculpture was in fact unveiled in June 2005 by Violet Wilson one of the oldest of the surviving screen lasses. The figures seem to be stepping out from a pillar of coal and the truly brilliant touch is that on the other side is a coal face worker down on his knees wielding a pick and it looks as if he is in the act of carving the other figures out of the coal. "Ninety percent looking and ten percent doing," as he once said to me. Well, in this case there was also another one hundred percent *thinking*.

From there it is only a short walk up to the Haig Mining Museum. The Haig, sunk during the First World War and so given its patriotic name, was the last of the deep mines to be worked in Cumberland and when it closed in 1986 it very nearly went the way of all the others in the area; the initial plan being to demolish it all to make way for a business enterprise park, but thankfully it was declared a Grade II building of architectural and historic interest and saved. A Pit Restoration Group took over the site in 1993 and since then volunteers have worked hard to preserve and restore what they can of the old building and engines. But there has been no tarting up. On a cold, wet day the pithead winding gear looks as grim as it must always have looked. The Bever Dorling winding engine has been fully restored to full working order and it is a massive piece of machinery. It is the size of everything that strikes you first, particularly the height of the ceilings. What always pleases me is that while there are some explanatory display boards, this again is a museum is full of *things*. There is the famous *Spedding Mill*, a lighting device invented in Whitehaven by Carlisle Spedding, the man who also designed St James's Church ! It produced a shower of sparks — safer by far than candles — by turning a hardened steel wheel against a flint, and it was in use for decades until the arrival of the Davy Lamp in 1816. Then there are modern lamps, boots, and knee pads, tally tokens, and of course the miners' picks and shovels. There are things as small and homely as the hookey mats the miners' wives made from rags, and as big as the *riding sets* — a kind of low-slung trolley-car — which carried groups of men quickly but uncomfortably to the coal face. Everything is there, presumably because everything was

Haig Mining Museum

just left there. And there are still ex-miners there, patiently ready to answer all the same old questions, even the daft ones.

And it was there that I bought a wonderful little book called *"Ah'd Gaa Back Tomorra!" Memories of West Cumbrian Screen Lasses.* Looking at the pictures tells you that the work was just as hard and as dirty as you could imagine, but reading it you soon learn what a pride they took in themselves. "I had a clean pinny on every day. My clogs were polished (and) we wore white scarves round our heads with a beret on top so just a thin white band showed to keep the dust off our hair." How happy they were. "I was really happy. It didn't matter about the hard work and getting dirty. Working on the screen was a 'prime time' of my life." And the fun they managed to have. "Sometimes the miners would send up dead mice with coal and, occasionally, there would be a message scratched on a piece of wood from a miner who fancied a particular screen lass."

There is a photograph of some of them on the front cover. They are wearing their white scarves and berets and though one or two look as though it would have been unwise to cross them, for the most part they do seem a very maternal group and while they are all buttoned up in their winter coats, there are plenty of warm smiles to be seen on their faces.

Continuing down the coast and just over the hill from the Mining Museum is Corkickle. *Corkickle?* It is such a silly sounding name. I suppose it is because I had the good fortune at Bristol University to have had as my tutor one of the most intellectually brilliant and the most entertaining men I have ever met — Basil Cottle, compiler of the *Penguin Dictionary of Surnames* — that I always want to know what a name means. And *Corkickle* indicates a settlement situated between a headland and a winding stream. It comes from two words: the Irish *Corr* meaning a point or headland and a Norse word *keekle* which is the winding stream. This blend of Irish and Norse is exactly what might be expected here as the Norsemen were driven out of Ireland in thirteenth century and settled over the water here in Cumberland. And there still is a River Keekle nearby and it certainly does twist and bend. Well, that may be the etymology of it, but for me Corkickle will always mean *Rugby League* as that's where Whitehaven play.

Having ended the chapter on Workington by remembering Bill Shankly, I thought I had better find out about something being played now, and knowing nothing about Rugby League I phoned Whitehaven's ground. Straightaway I was invited to spend a match day with them and to have lunch with the sponsors and the directors. Now the Directors Dining Room at Whitehaven may be only a series of Portacabins, which in material terms might seem a little humble, but in terms of warmth of hospitality, it is palatial. And they serve a very good lunch. Des Byrne, the Club Chairman, welcomed me and though obviously busy, spared time to tell me about the club and to sit me down next to its President, Richard Woodall, of whom more, much more in a later chapter.

To make sure I understood what was going on, when the match began I was given a seat alongside Paul Newton who would have been commentating on the game for Radio Cumbria if his machinery had been working. As it wasn't, he talked to me and sent occasional reports in to Carlisle on his mobile phone.

I suppose the only thing I did know about Rugby League was the name Eddie Waring, the Yorkshireman who used to commentate on the game in the 60's and whose distinctive voice everybody thought they could imitate. So I don't think I ever took it seriously. As Paul said, "Below the M62 it's off the radar." I think I had a sort of subconscious notion that it was a brutal sort of game played by cauliflower-eared northerners with beer-bellies. When the teams came out on the pitch I saw how very wrong I had been. These were athletes. That was muscle. And how they moved — so nimble, so fleet of foot, and over short distances such explosive acceleration. It was a much more open and elegant game than rugby union — none of those interminable rucks and mauls and heaps of bodies and brute strength. This was skill. And no one argued with the referee, I noticed. I was told that simply wasn't done. And no prima donnas. These were mostly local lads, playing for a few hundred pounds. Many of them seemingly worked at Sellafield and some might even be going straight to work after the game. There was one brief fight on the pitch. Punches were thrown, but Paul dismissed it. "Handbags," he said, "just handbags."

In the second half there was a piece of play which really did impress me. On as a substitute came Neil Baynes. He weighs eighteen stone and is built, I think the saying is, (I hope he will forgive me; yes, he is so big I do hope he forgives me) built like a brick shit-house. Given the ball, Mr Baynes ran in a dead straight line and it took three, if not four Doncaster players to bring him down, so leaving a huge hole in their defence. A couple of quick passes and one of the nimble-footed crew was in under the posts for a simple try and Neil Baynes was heading back to the touchline. Job done!

We won. I say *we,* as Whitehaven were my team now and always will be. We beat Doncaster by 22-12 and after the match Des Byrne asked me, as someone new to the game, to draw the raffle ticket. To my horror, I drew out my own number. I had won a signed match ball. I was about to hand it back, but looking around I saw people smiling as though they thought it was only right. I took it home with me, but I wasn't totally sure though and next time I saw Richard Woodall I gave it to him and asked him to give it to some young supporter.

Six:

Coastal path. Flowers and seabirds. Guillemots.
The lighthouse. Pete Laver. Fleswick Bay. St Bees.
Coast to Coast Walk. St Bega. Midsummer snow.
The Priory. Josefina de Vasconcellos. Theological
College. Rev James Jackson. A body is found. St
Bees School. Barring out. Visitors Guide.

I suppose I really should by now have pointed out that there is a designated Coastal Path running from Gretna, north of Carlisle, as far south as Silverdale and Morecambe Bay, but as much of the northern part, especially around Maryport and Workington, is rather drab, it hasn't seemed worth while. Once past Whitehaven though the landscape

Colin Telfer's "St. Bega" at St. Bees.

suddenly changes. It is here, where the coalfields stop and the sandstone begins, that mining and heavy industry give way to agriculture and you don't have to go far along the footpath before there are fields with cows and sheep in them. It seems almost symbolic now that just as the green fields start to appear, if you look over to your left there are the rusting, dilapidated skeletons of buildings which had once been part of a major industrial site. Albright and Wilson were leaders in the field of chemical engineering and employed over three thousand people here until falling profits and a series of hostile take-over bids forced them into closure in 2002. Now it is just a mess, and I can't se anyone declaring it to be of special historical interest and wanting to preserve it for posterity. The sooner it is bulldozed into oblivion the better.

The further along the path you go, so there are more and more flowers to be seen; buttercup and red clover, gorse and foxglove. I wonder if it's true that the pattern inside the mouth of each individual foxglove is different. It is said to be true of snowflakes and there must be far more of them. There is the soft blue of sheep's-bit too, which seems appropriate, and lower down on the cliff face bank after pink bank of thrift. Thrift is the flower which used to be on the reverse side of the old twelve-sided threepenny bit and was either some kind of pun or the Royal Mint hadn't got their facts straight, as the name has nothing at all to do with money or thriftiness; it comes instead from an Old English word meaning *to thrive* which is exactly what it does. Even after it dies the flowers stay on, pale and papery. I like the comment about it in Gerard's *Herball* (1597) "Their use in Physicke as yet is not knowne." That all plants had some use was obvious to his way of thinking and they would find one eventually.

But it is sea birds that this cliff walk is most famous for: guillemots and razorbills, kittiwakes and fulmars. Sailing and turning on the thermals, the fulmars are a wonderful sight, but the name means *foul gull*, as when they are disturbed or threatened, they squirt out an evil-smelling and oily mess from tubes on top of their beaks. It is the guillemots which are the main attraction though. Nine thousand pairs nest here, Dave Blackledge tells me.

Now for a long time (until about twenty minutes ago to be quite honest, when I thought I had better check it out) I thought that guillemots

116

was also the French word for quotation marks. I was close: it's *guillemets*. I though I had remembered it from my French dictation exercises at Grammar School: *point et virgule; deux points.* I even justified it to myself by saying that this was how the French saw them, as two pairs of guillemots, upright and with their long beaks turned in towards the words. All right, laugh if you want. I can still see it though, and I wish I was right. Guillemots does come from a French word anyway, according to Francesca Greenoak in her marvellous book *All The Birds of the Air;* well, if not actually French, Breton: *gwelan.*

Nine thousand nesting pairs. You can smell them long before you see them. When the chicks are almost ready to fly there isn't an inch of space left on any of the ledges; they are like iron filings on a magnet. How the parent birds, bringing fish and sand eels home for their young from out in the Irish Sea, don't get their heads splattered against the rock face when there is an inshore gale blowing I will never know and how do they know which chick is theirs?

Eventually, the time comes for the young to leave their nest, if you can call a bare shelf of rock a nest. The adults fly off first and call to them from down on the sea And then they have to jump. I don't know how many hundred feet it is, but it's a long way, especially when it's the first step you have ever taken. They go just as the evening light is fading so as to try and avoid the skuas and the herring gulls. Not all of them are lucky. You jump off into space and then you are eaten. An eventful life and a short one.

Given the chance, herring gulls really are serial killers. I took my two daughters to the gullery on Walney Island when they were little and we hadn't been there for more than a few minutes when one chick, a dear little fluffy thing, wandered six inches or so out of the safety zone of its own nest and a neighbouring gull simply reached out and swallowed it whole. There was a moment of shocked silence, then a wail of tears. "It ate it!" There was no way of saving the day after that bit of cannibalism.

On a windy day, and there are plenty of windy days along the cliff top, if you are looking for somewhere sheltered to have your sandwiches, then the best thing is to head for the lighthouse and get down behind the wall. There has been a lighthouse on St Bees Head since 1718. That first one, built by Thomas Lutwige was a sturdy sandstone tower about thirty feet high. It didn't have a lamp of any kind though. On top was a metal grate onto which the keepers tipped loads of coal, and damned hard work it must have been getting it up there. Even so, there were always complaints as on wet and windy nights there tended to be more smoke than fire which wasn't a lot of use. Nevertheless, it lasted like that until 1822, when, not surprisingly, it burned down. Trinity House then erected the handsome building that is there today and the light was oil-fired. Not any longer of course, and it isn't manned now either, but operated automatically from Trinity House Operations Centre at Harwich.

I never walk this path without thinking of a much-loved and much-missed friend, Pete Laver. He was Librarian of Dove Cottage and can be credited with turning the old museum into the exciting Exhibition Centre it is today. He was also a gifted poet in his own right and great fun to be with. Sadly he died of a heart attack on Scafell while out walking in August 1983. And he was only thirty-six. Considering the pace at which he lived perhaps we should not have been surprised, but his friends were devastated. Why I remember him especially on this path is because of a dream he once told me about. He dreamed he was in Dove Cottage and Wordsworth came in, so, seizing the opportunity, Pete said to him, "Mr Wordsworth…" Well, you would have to, wouldn't you? You wouldn't dare address him as William. "Mr Wordsworth," said Pete, "which is your own favourite among all your poems?" And Wordsworth replied, "Stanzas Suggested in a Steamboat off Saint Bees' Heads," And Pete paused a moment and said to me, "And I didn't know if he was joking." Now Wordsworth was never known as someone wont to set the table on a roar, but this time he must have been joking. It must have been a flash of merriment. Surely? It was a poem he wrote in 1833, not one of his vintage years and it drones on for nineteen stanzas – over one hundred and sixty eminently forgettable lines.

I have one other vivid memory of Pete. We had been out walking together and there was something he was trying to remember from Dorothy Wordsworth's *Journal*, so when we got back to Grasmere he went into the museum, unlocked the glass case and looked it up in the actual journal. I was so shocked to see what he was doing that I can't remember what we were looking for now.

This cliff top walk is one I have done many times and one of the most beautiful parts of it ought to be Fleswick Bay. Well, the Bay itself *is*; it is the way down which has become so squalid. High seas and winds have blown hundreds of plastic bottles and other bits of garbage into the tight little gorge that leads down to it. Much of it is now firmly stuck between the rocks and getting slimy. And it stinks. But brave it out and get down onto the beach; it is well worth it. This was once, so it's said, where the smugglers bringing brandy from the Isle of Man landed their small boats, and I can well believe it. Nowadays though it almost always quiet and deserted and beautiful. The sandstone cliffs rise up sheer above you and over the years people have carved their names into the soft stone. Some of the nineteenth century ones are so expertly done you would think they had all been stone masons. And as for *Frederick Furneaux Eversfield*, looking at where his name is, he must have lowered himself down on a sling in 1866. I am told that the name *Nat Lofthouse* is also featured there, but, if it is, and I haven't seen it myself, I do have my doubts that the great Bolton Wanderers striker did it himself. It was more likely an act of homage on some supporter's part, but what homage!

When you look down on the beach from the cliff top it looks to be black as though it is larva, but in fact it is made up of tiny pieces of gravel. People come there to search for agates and other semi-precious stones. I am not sure exactly what constitutes a *semi-precious* stone. Is it, I wonder, that they become precious once you have agreed to pay the exorbitant prices asked by the people who polish them and string them together as bracelets? And *semi* because they are suddenly worth precious little if you try to sell them back again? No, perish such a cynical thought.

Half way between Fleswick Bay and St. Bees itself, at a point marked on the map as Tomlin, there are what are known as *Pattering Holes*, holes which are said to lead down into a series of subterranean caverns where local smugglers would store their contraband prior to distributing it inland. Anthony Reeve, the Head of Classics at St. Bees School, tells me that in 1908 a master called Emil Zullig roped himself up and went down deep into one and found a "huge iron-bound door" which he couldn't move. There is no way of checking this out now unfortuneately as the holes are blocked with various bits of debris and the corpses of unlucky sheep. Legend also has it that the smugglers had an underground tunnel leading from the cliffs into the churchyard, but considering how water-logged the ground is there, it is hard to believe, and it is by no means the only coastal church with such a "tunnel".

When you get to the last rise before starting to go downhill into St Bees there is the remains of a little coastguard lookout post with engraved outline sketches naming the hills you can see in each direction if the weather is clear enough. The last time I was there the weather was foul, and I couldn't see any of them, but I was rewarded with the sight of a stonechat keeping sentinel on a spire of gorse. You hear them before you see them. *Tchek tchek.* It is just like two pebbles being clicked together. The stonechat has always been a bit special for me as it was the first unusual bird I ever identified. Identified with the aid of Edmund Sanders *A Bird Book for the Pocket.* I still have it on my bookshelf, even though I don't use it any more. It was a Christmas present form my mother when I was ten and it cost 12/6 and so was fairly expensive. There have been better bird books by the dozen since, but then it was special, and not least because one of the *Swallows and Amazon* boys had used it in my favourite Arthur Ransome novel, *Great Northern?* I poured over its pages for hours until I am sure that by the age of eleven I could probably have identified any bird in Britain — as long as it was facing to the left!

Standing on the last headland you have a very mixed view in front of you. The towers of Sellafield to the south and at your feet row after row of static caravans, more static caravans than there are houses in the town it would seem. Totally regimented they are: dead straight lines and each with its shiny Calor Gas cylinder standing at the door, as bright and upright as guardsmen. But where are all the people? It always seems so eerily deserted.

No, this is decidedly not the best direction from which to approach St Bees, as beyond the caravans you are faced with a vast expanse of car park, which may well be seething at weekends, but has never had more than a handful of cars in it when I've been there, nor have I ever seen any dogs using the sandy 'toilet area' kindly provided for them by the council. You might though see someone with a rucksack on their back heading in the direction you just came from, in which case they are in all likelihood setting out on the Coast to Coast Walk, the 190 mile trail which Wainwright introduced in the 1970's. Over the Pennines, down Swaledale and across the North York Moors it goes to Robin Hood's Bay.

But if you keep on trudging in the direction you were heading and pass the drab façade of the Ship Inn ("Is there anybody there?" said the traveller.) and come nearer to the town itself, things do begin to change. For one, there is another piece of sculpture by Colin Telfer: the slim, girlish figure of St. Bega standing beside her coracle, and if you look closely you will notice – a nice touch this – that she seems to have caught the hem of her dress as she stepped ashore and a little bit of it is draped over the side of the tiny boat.

St. Bega was a Irish girl, living in the tenth century, at the same time as St. Hilda of Whitby. She was the daughter of an Irish king, and arrangements had been put in hand for her to marry the King of Norway. A wise political move on her father's part, but Bega had vowed to remain a virgin and to lead a totally ascetic life, in token of which an angel had given her a bracelet decorated with a cross. Interestingly, *Sancta Bega* is ecclesiastic Latin for the Old English *halgan beage,* or *holy bracelet,* so it is open to question whether her name suggested that she had such a bracelet, or whether the existence of such a bracelet suggested that there must have been such a saint. Some have certainly doubted her existence. Whichever, she is seen to be wearing it on Colin's statue, and such a bracelet was actually preserved as a relic in St. Bees and records show that oaths were sworn on it as late as 1279, but in 1315 the Scots invaded the town and they must have made off with it as it is never mentioned again.

Clearly Bega never had any intention of marrying anyone, not even if he was King of Norway, but how to get out of the situation she found herself in? On the night before her wedding, brave colleen that she was, she stole a coracle and fled alone across the Irish Sea to England, landing, probably, at Fleswick Bay and making her way up the cliff path and along the headland to what is now the town named after her. Here she achieved what she really wanted; she became a nun, receiving the veil, so the story goes, from St. Aidan of Lindisfarne himself.

She could have become an anchorite, a hermit, but Bega had been a royal princess. She was used to having people around her and what she wanted was to establish a convent, so she asked the Lord of Egremont if he would grant her some land on which to build one. Contemptuously, he said she could have as much of his land as would be covered by snow the next day – which just happened to be Midsummer's Day. He really ought to have known better. This was a future saint he was being snotty to and besides he was living in Cumberland where such things don't only happen in stories. In this story, when Midsummer Morning dawned there was a three mile stretch of land covered in snow. Bega had her convent.

There is no trace of it whatsoever now, but on the same site, it is safe to assume, a Benedictine Priory was built, possibly as early as 1120 by William de Meschin, who dedicated it – no fall of snow was needed this time – to St. Bega. During the reign of Henry VIII it suffered the same fate as many other great religious houses and was pulled down in 1539, only the chapel allowed to survive and become the parish church.

The arch of its west door with its successive arcades of zigzag ornamentation and its "beakheads" of grotesque birds, or they might be beasts, dates from 1160 and is the oldest surviving part of the Priory, but in a niche in the wall opposite the door is something which is possibly even older – a "dragon stone", thought to be from the lintel of a Norman building. It was found in the 1860's when the south aisle wall was being rebuilt and it shows the "war in heaven", when "Michael and his angels fought against the dragon." But does it? The beast might just as well be Fafnir, the dragon of Norse mythology which was slain by Sigurd when it was guarding the treasure of Hreidmor, the Dwarf King. Indeed , there is no reason why it might not be both. As on the Gosforth Cross, which we will come to soon, whoever carved it might well have been hedging his bets on the 'truths' of religion.

Commemorated inside the priory church is another version of the St. Bega story, according to which the moment she landed on the Cumberland coast she looked up and saw a vision of Mary holding the infant Jesus in her arms, and this scene is depicted in two extraordinarily moving statues in the Lady Chapel. Mary is holding the child out – almost offering it to the kneeling figure of a very young, indeed girlish Bega, and while the two figures are separate, with the altar between them, the *communication* between them is almost tangible. They are the work of Josefina de Vasconcellos. The daughter of a Brazilian diplomat, Josefina de Vasconcellos was born in London in 1904, but lived most of her life in a remote and tiny farmhouse in Little Langdale. Her work can be found in churches and cathedrals the length and breadth of the country, from

Maryport to Norwich, and Edinburgh to St. Paul's, but she stayed true to representational art and so never achieved the acclaim and popularity of her contemporaries such as Barbara Hepworth and Henry Moore. And today as Linda Clifford observes in her study of the artist, "Critics find it easier to look at a dead sheep preserved in formaldehyde than assess a sculpture that represents someone's ideas of religion, sentiments or emotions such as Love."

Inside, the church is not very interesting; most of it is the result of the usual Victorian vandalism, but outside, at the east end, the medieval chancel remains. It was re-roofed and given a totally new lease of life in 1816. In those early years of the nineteenth century, when towns were expanding and the population was beginning to grow and grow, new churches were being built all the time, but one of the problems was that there were hardly enough trained clergy to meet the new demands. The tuition at Oxford and Cambridge had not changed for generations and was predominantly academic, which meant abstruse dissertations and Latin and Greek. It was somewhat out of touch and it was also out of the reach, both socially and financially, of the average young man who felt he had a vocation. Something new was needed, and so it was that in 1816 the country's first independent Church of England Theological College was opened in St. Bees. Wordsworth welcomed it, as could be expected, with some heavy-footed verses ending

> Oh may that power who hushed the stormy seas,
> And cleared a way for the first votaries,
> Prosper the new-born College of St. BEES!

And indeed it did prosper. A house was built for the Principal and the Chancel of the old priory church was repaired and fitted out as a lecture room and library. Over the years more than 2600 clergy were trained there and at one time it had more than 100 students. It was not cheap either. Fees were £10 per term with three guineas added "for repairs and library". The course lasted for two years and as Reay's *Guide* tells us the students had to buy their own books, their cap and gown and they had to find their own lodgings in the town, which could cost them around £1 a week.

It was an innovation and innovations are not always popular. In 1826 there was a wonderfully weird and snobbish outcry against it in the *Westmoreland Gazette*. "[whoever] should enter almost any village in the diocese of Chester, he is sure to meet with an ostentatious coxcomb of a Curate, half-mannered and scarcely half-educated, who with great care and attention has pursued the knowledge of Classics and Divinity for the lengthened period of six months… this man will point to St. Bees as the seat of his education…and boast of his far learned nothingness. This institution can teach the awkward peasant good manners and the green-grocer good breeding…[but]..the seabird screams shame upon thee; the sea surge dashing its spray on the neighbouring rocks, mingles with the howling blast in a threat against thee. Thou art a passport into the Church for the ignorant, and those brought up in secular employment… and deprivest the well educated of a situation." Some pompous and "well-educated" sour grapes behind this, by the sound of it.

But its independence and not prejudice was ultimately its downfall. Privately financed by the Principal, it was in effect a business and when regulations were introduced which demanded that the College should be affiliated to a University, it found itself out on a limb and a geographically remote limb at that. Numbers fell, the Principal faced financial ruin and it was finally closed in 1895. Today it serves as a parish hall and is also used by St. Bees School as a music room.

Muscular Christianity was a term much in vogue when the College was flourishing and there can hardly have been a better exponent of it than the Rev. James Jackson who is buried in the churchyard nearby. Born in 1796 in Millom, he first fought against Napoleon and then decided he would take up arms for Christ. He trained at St. Bees College and was vicar of Rivington near Preston until 1856 when he retired to Cumberland and took up rock climbing. No nylon ropes then, no cleats or crampons, no Rock Boots. You hammered some nails into the soles of your second best boots, wrapped a scarf round you neck if it chanced to feel a bit chilly and off you went. He was seventy-nine was James Jackson when he first climbed Pillar Rock in Ennerdale. That was in 1875. Next year, to celebrate his eightieth birthday, he set off at 4.20 am, by himself, climbed it again and was back at Ritson's Hotel in time for lunch. But his third attempt proved to be his last. It was April 30th 1878. He fell and was killed. Maybe it was how he would have liked to go, but it was three days before they found his body. He had once written of himself:

If this in your mind you will fix,

124

When I make the Pillar my toy,
I was born in 1, 7, 9, 6,
And you'll think me a nimble old boy.
Yes, I think we would all agree with that.

There was one other remarkable interment at St.Bees, but no one knew anything about it until 1981, when a group of archaeologists from Leicester University, unable to dig where they had planned to as heavy rain was flooding their trenches, moved to a drier site closer to the church where an extension had been built about 1300 but later abandoned. What they found was a stone-lined vault with a female skeleton on the north side and a lead coffin to the south. It was somewhat crushed so they were not expecting to find anything in it, at best a skeleton, at worst something slimy. When they did open it what they discovered was a linen 'parcel', shaped like a person and tied up with string. Luckily, they managed to rush it to a hospital mortuary where apparently the admissions paper-work caused a bit of a problem, but no damage had been done. In fact the linen shroud had been so impregnated with beeswax that no air or damp had ever managed to penetrate it, so what with that and the lead coffin, what they had when the 'parcel' was unwrapped was the perfectly preserved body of a man between thirty-five and forty-five years old. So preserved was it, that Dr Tapp, a pathologist from Preston Royal Infirmary declared he would be able to perform a 'routine autopsy'. The skin was so intact you could have taken his finger-prints. There was stubble on his chin and he had a good head of hair, but most remarkable of all his internal organs and body tissue were so well preserved that they were still pink when cut. He had not been in the best of health though. The autopsy revealed several dental abscesses which must have been very painful and he had sinus trouble. Far more serious however was a double fracture of the jaw-bone and a fractured rib, the broken end of which had punctured his left lung and would inevitably have been the cause of death. He might, it was thought, have fallen from his horse, but the injury to his jaw-bone looked more like the result of a fight - a battle.

There was no inscription on the lead coffin, so no way of knowing for sure who he was. Clearly he had been a man of some importance and there had never been that many powerful families in the area. Two stone effigies within the church and which might at some time have been positioned above the vault suggested either Anthony de Lucy, Lord of Cockermouth and Egremont, but he had died fighting abroad, or Sir Robert Harrington, who was known to have been buried in St. Bees in 1297. He had married a wealthy heiress, so was hers the female skeleton? His effigy looks exactly like any other effigy of the time so there is no way of knowing. When he was reburied, on 21st August 1981, with all due ceremony, he was called 'our brother unknown'.

The abbeys and priories of pre-Reformation England were by no means all dens of idleness, corruption and luxury as Henry VIII's spin doctors led people to believe and when they were done away with, the poor, and not only the poor, found themselves with nowhere to go for skilled medical treatment and certainly nowhere where they could get a free education.

Some of them had been very fine schools, and the school at St.Bees must have been particularly so during the first half of the sixteenth century, as two little boys who went there at the same time and were taught together, both went on to become archbishops of the Reformed Church of England.

Edwin Sandys became Archbishop of York in 1576, succeeding his former school-friend Edward Grindall who had been appointed Archbishop of Canterbury.

Grindall must have valued his education at the Priory and though a prelate of the new Church of England, he was sufficiently aware of what losses reform had brought about that he founded a free grammar school to ensure that the children of the area might still have the benefits he had known. Founded in 1583, it was ready to admit its first pupils in 1588, the year of the Armada. That first schoolroom is still there to the north of the main gateway and is exactly what you would expect Dickens' Dotheboys Hall to have been like. You can almost hear the echoes of the thrashings some Cumbrian Whackford Squeers would have handed out here. Long and wood-panelled, it is now a dining room, but there are names carved into almost every inch of it: *L.S Proctor* having been most meticulous in the carving of his. Didn't anyone see him doing it?

There are other and sadder names recorded in the Chapel. 184 Old Boys of the School died in the First World War. A terrible number for such a small school. Three were awarded the Victoria Cross — one, Captain

W. Leefe Robinson having shot down the first zeppelin, over London, at night and flying with no instrumentation.

It was the ubiquitous Lowther family who quite unintentionally provided the school with many of its main buildings. The school had leased the mineral rights of their land to them in 1742 for eight hundred and seventy-six years at the ludicrous sum of £3.10s a year. Long and protracted legal proceedings ended with the Lowther family having to hand over £5,000, which, wisely invested, jumped to £30,000 and gave the school many of the elegant sandstone buildings it is graced with today.

The author of the School History described it as having 'an atmosphere of undeniable calm and steadfastness, a sort of aura of piety and faith in great things.' That may not be quite how we would put it today, but I do know what he means. The school has not always displayed such calm though, and certainly not in the early years of the eighteenth century. There was a tradition which lasted until 1760 known as *Barring Out*. It took place at the beginning of Lent and consisted of preventing the Master and his Usher from entering the school until they had agreed to a list of 'rights' the pupils wanted for the coming year. Mostly it was a good-humoured affair, but not so, it seems, in 1706. Things must have got seriously out of hand as the Master himself set down in writing a number of terms and conditions which the pupils were to abide by. One reads, "That they carry themselves civilly to all Persons that pass by, and that no Pistols be shot at Persons that ride by on Horse-back, much less ye Master or Usher of this free Gramar (sic) school, and that those rude Boys that act to ye Contrary be exposed to condign punishment."

Pistols! We should be careful how we criticise the 'youth of today'.

Perhaps it is because it is home to so many public school masters — and mistresses, girls being admitted in 1976 — that St. Bees seems so sedate today, not to say twee. I noticed that number 123 Main Street is called *Yan Tan Tetherer.* There is really no need for that.

The Visitor's Guide to St. Bees, published by John Reay about in 1869 calls St. Bees "this little northern Athens". That's as maybe; he lived there and had his fingers in several commercial pies, but for all that there is nothing quite like the advertisements in the back pages of these old local guide books for giving a brief and vivid insight into how people were living. They are a mine of social history. Hotel proprietors, for instance, show a degree of deference which we would never meet with today. Jas. Muncaster of *The Wheatsheaf* in Egremont "Begs to thank his numerous patrons for past favors (sic)," while Daniel Tyson of the *Scawfell Hotel* in Seascale expresses "his thanks for the liberal support he has received during the many years he has been the Proprietor of this Hotel and respectfully intimates that many improvements have been made." What tourists expected from these hotels has changed somewhat too. William Ritson of the *Wastwater Hotel* assures his guests that "Post Horses, Mountain Ponies, Wheeled Carriages, Guides, Postboys and Boatmen, etc., are always in readiness." The drivers can always be relied upon to be "steady". F. Minton Haines, M.A., of Christ College, Cambridge, was running a Boarding School for the Sons of Gentlemen at Distington, where "its healthy position renders it particularly suitable for delicate boys." For those adults who were of a delicate disposition, John Reay's Chemists in St. Bees offered a bewildering array of domestic medicines. Laudanum, of course, but also other exotic potions, such as Opodeldoc, Ipecacuanah, and Tincture of Turkey Rhubarb. You could not be too careful in your dealings with the medical world though in those days and *The Whitehaven News* assured its readers that "Objectionable Medical Advertisements (were) Excluded". What? But, never mind, Glenlivat Whisky could be bought in Whitehaven for 17/- a gallon. That's about 75p. Or there was Quinine Sherry. I like the sound of that too. And Mr. Reay could always sell you a perfume called *Kiss Me Quietly and Forget Me Not.* So clearly life in St.Bees did have its skittish moments.

Seven:

Braystones. Jack Henson. Braystones Tower.
Beckermet. Wotobank. St Bridget's. Sellafield.
Calder Hall. Windscale. The fire. The Visitors'
Centre. Chernobyl. Gosforth. The hogback tombs
and the Gosforth Cross.

I never travel up or down the coast on the train without my eye being caught by the houses which line the shore at Nethertown, just south of St Bees, or again at Braystones. Some are little more than beach huts, one or two are just shacks, but for the most part they look to be substantial bungalows and more are being built. What must it be like, I have often wondered, to live down there. Wonderful sunsets from your front window,

Above: The Gosforth Cross

there would be. But who owned the land, and how did anyone ever get permission to build so close to the sea, literally on the beach? And who were the first?

It has been suggested that immigrant workers in the mines, looking for somewhere to live, might well have established some kind of squat there as far back as the eighteenth century, but if they did they left no trace of themselves behind which has not been cleared away or swept out to sea. In a sketch of Braystones Railway Station published in the Illustrated London News in 1850 there is only the station house to be seen, but by the beginning of last century bungalows had begun to appear, and in the 1911-1912 edition of his *Directory* Bulmer is declaring that Braystones is "becoming known as a health resort". And it certainly was in the years between the wars when it was the "professional classes" who frequented it.

Most of the early development seems to have been to the south of the station, which today is the more run-down area: derelict caravans, abandoned tractors, rusting bikes and old tyres. And inevitably there are yards and yards of orange bailer twine and an assortment of rubber gloves. They always seem to be getting washed up, but the garden roller — big enough to roll out a cricket pitch — could certainly not have been washed up. It's hard to know what that is doing there on a shingle beach. Councils can not have been so particular about planning regulations in the years just after the last war as apparently there were two buses down there and at least one old railway carriage, all being lived in at one time.

The area has known its share of accidents over the years. Several wooden buildings have burned down, which is hardly surprising as it is a long and twisting way to the nearest fire station. One however was always rumoured to have been an insurance scam and another was simply an act of wanton vandalism. It was here too in July 1977 that a train from Marchon Chemical Works — a diesel pulling ten 100-ton wagons behind it — proved to be too heavy for one of the smaller bridges it was crossing and it collapsed. The train was derailed and wagons slid down the embankment, crushing one house completely and demolishing most of another. Both, as luck would have it, were empty when it happened.

The sea too can be a destroyer. In the great storm of 2nd February 2002 a bungalow called *Braesurf* was smashed beyond repair. Waves went over and through the roof and boulders as big as footballs were sent crashing through its windows. Fortunately again, Mike and Catherine Rogers were not at home. Even more fortunately they were fully insured and the new *Braesurf* is one of the most elegant and delightful bungalows along the whole of the beach. I think I could see myself living there — listening to the sound of the sea, watching the sunsets and slowly reading my way through the whole of Henry James.

The Braystones bungalows must have been home to a few *characters* over the years and they still are. If you were to stop at the *Lobster-Pot* and had an hour or so (at least) to spare, then Jack Henson, who has lived there since 1964, would tell you some tales. There was the man whose roof blew off and he carried on watching the television. And the old lady who died and the undertakers could not get their hearse along the shingle so Jack kindly carried her coffin to them on the back of his tractor. And then there was Jennet Crouch. A policeman knocked on her door one night to say that the Post Office at Drigg had been broken into and they were looking for a man. "Looking for a man?" she said. "I've been looking for one for years, and if one broke in here, I'd lock him in."

Jack is clearly in his element there. As he said to me, all he needs to live on is a bag of dripping and some spuds; there's enough fish in the sea. He isn't, as he admitted, big on vegetarianism.

Walking inland towards Braystones Village and towards Beckermet you pass the Tarnside Caravan Park with its row upon row of 'static caravans'. So very orderly and so very soulless. I very much doubt if any eccentricity is tolerated there.

But the village itself does have a folly of its own: *Braystones Tower.* A slim, stone-built, turreted tower, three storeys high, it looks as if it were once part of a great and ancient manor house, but it never was. As its inscription proclaims, *"In Honour of the Queen and in commemoration of the Diamond Jubilee — sixty years' reign 1837-1897 — of Her Majesty Queen Victoria of Great Britain and Ireland, this tower was erected by William Henry Watson of Braystones."* An earlier member of the family, William Hough Watson, an industrial chemist, had hit on the idea of using vegetable oil instead of the usual tallow and so invented the more attractive product they called *Sunlight Soap.* His boss, who of course got most of the credit, went on to become Lord Leverhume, but William did nicely out of it and retired to Braystones.

The tower once housed Watson's museum of curiosities, ranging from a Neolithic quern to a collection of sea shells and cannon used at Waterloo. Time was when, on Empire Day, with the Union Flag flying from the top of the tower, the public were allowed inside to view it all. But he died in 1934 and the ritual opening stopped in the mid 1940's. The building, having been vandalised, it is a sad and isolated sight now, held prisoner behind a barbed wire fence. But looking at it as you leave the village, and with the giant towers of Sellafield behind it, some might be prompted to ask which is the greater folly.

Beckermet, as its name suggests. is a place where two becks — the Black Beck and Kirk Beck — meet. It is a quiet little village and the only interesting things about it are both to be found some distance outside it. To the northeast is an earthworks marked on the OS map as a Castle, but it never was a castle in the accepted sense of the word and there is no evidence that there was ever any stone building there. Its location would rather suggest some sort of raised defensive position possibly dating back to early British times, but after the Norman Conquest we do know that William gave it to Sir Michael de Fleming, together with the manor of Aldingham in Furness where there is a similar motte and bailey mound. The Flemings seem to have abandoned it some time in the middle of the thirteenth century, and confusingly there are family records which call it Caernarvon Castle, but that British/Welsh name appears to mean no more than a stronghold opposite an island. In this case the Isle of Man, not Anglesey.

Someone I stopped and talked to in Beckermet told me a story which is obviously ludicrous (he thought as much himself) but I will pass it on nevertheless. There is a hill nearby called Wotobank which got its name, so the legend goes, because a lord of Beckermet was out hunting with his wife and they became separated. After a long and painful search she was found lying on this hill, or bank, with a wolf in the very act of tearing the poor lady to pieces. Her husband, naturally distraught, is then said to have called out, "Woe to this bank!" Why he didn't call out, "Woe to my wife!" or "Get that bloody wolf!", the story does not explain. Anyway, it allowed a certain Mrs Cowley, I have since found, to write a poem called *Edwina* which contains the lines:

132

"Woe to thee, bank!" th'attendants echoed round,
And pitying shepherds caught the grief-fraught sound,
Thus to this hour, through ev'ry changing age,
Through ev'ry year's still ever-varying stage,
The name remains. and *Woto-bank* is seen
From ev'ry mountain bleak, and valley green;
Dim Skiddaw views it from its monstrous height,
And eagles mark it in their dizzy flight.
And nobody could argue with that.

To the west, a mile at least from the village itself and down a long narrow lane that gets badly flooded in wet weather, is Beckermet's oldest church, St. Bridget's. It dates from the thirteenth century and though services are still occasionally held there, it has not really been in use for over a century. Hence it is almost a time capsule. The wooden pews are ancient and look very uncomfortable. It is damp and smelly and feels somehow to be such a sad place. So little has changed over the years that the Royal Coat of Arms over the altar is that of George III. Either side of it are painted the Lord's Prayer and the Creed — so dispensing with the need for prayer and hymn books I suppose — and on the north wall are the Ten Commandments. The altar itself is a simple stone slab on which are carved five small crosses symbolising the five wounds of Christ. It is worth a visit if only because it has such an aura of Hardyesque melancholy to it. In the graveyard, which is full of purple crocus in February, are two truncated stumps of Saxon crosses, but so weathered that it is really only possible to make out the interlace. There are some words too, but they are so worn away that it is not even clear to me what language they are written in. And as if the melancholy wasn't enough, the church's two fifteenth century bells were stolen in 2002. Thankfully though, after a lot of publicity and appeals they reappeared — no one knows where from or how — six months later, but damaged of course. Local feeling was such that several businesses paid to have them refurbished and they are now back in place. Death knells, I would imagine, are probably their forte.

The Watson family of Braystones are buried here and it is just possible to catch sight of the top of Braystones Tower as you head back up the lane. There is also a nice view of Sellafield from the graveyard.

I can't remember now why it was that shortly after I first came to live in Cumbria, back in the late 70's, I found myself outside the main gates of BNFL at Sellafield. Curiosity most likely. But I do remember that a local building company must have been contracted to do some work on the site at that time, and so, displayed alongside the entrance, and with those infamous towers as a backdrop, there was a board bearing the company's name in large capital letters: EDEN. Dante's inscription over those other gates *Lasciate ogni speranza, voi ch'entrate* (Abandon hope, all you who enter here) might have been more appropriate in those days of CND, but were we to go back a further fifty years, into the 1920's, then no such irony would have been detected. Radiation held no fears for people then. This was a major leap forward for mankind. This was the very forefront of the advancement of science, where man was seen to be harnessing (I have always liked that somewhat agricultural metaphor) the power of nature. The bright beacon pointing the way to all kinds of blessings and prosperity was *Radium*. Old advertisements of the time show us that there was Radium toothpaste. Even Radium shoe polish. Not that any of these products was in any way radioactive; it is simply that the word itself had become the latest selling factor, much as the word *organic* is today. I would not be surprised if there weren't *Organic Toothpaste* on sale somewhere. But, at the same time, there were genuinely radioactive "health drinks" to be had and people drank them, urged on by one Eben Byers, a fanatic and internationally renowned businessman, who, sadly, but hardly surprisingly, died of radiation poisoning. What is surprising is that this Brave New World attitude to radioactivity survived the bombing of Hiroshima and Nagasaki.

In 1956, when the Queen officially opened the first nuclear reactor at Calder Hall and it was connected to the National Grid, flags flew, crowds cheered, and bands played. The spin doctors of the day came up with the brilliant sound bite that nuclear electricity would soon be "too cheap to meter" and there were promises of such things as nuclear-powered cars! What a golden future it heralded.

As the earliest Ordnance Survey Maps show, there were once two tiny hamlets — you could not have called them villages — Low Sellafield and High Sellafield, some rough grazing on the Cumberland plain and a deer park belonging to Calder Abbey, but in 1941 the area was bought by the war-time Ministry of Supply and a factory was set up to produce TNT which was then transported down the coast to Drigg where shells and bombs were made. So there has long been as aura of secrecy and suspicion about the place and this only increased when the war was over and the atomic bombs had been dropped by the Americans. The Cold War was starting, but British scientists were no longer welcome at American nuclear research sites, so it was then that the Prime Minister, Clement Atlee, decided that this country should have its own independent nuclear deterrent, as he saw it, to balance world power. What was needed for the research and development was a location far enough away from any large conurbation, yet one with a large labour pool. A coastal area was also favoured and one which had a plentiful supply of pure water. The script seemed to have been written for Sellafield, particularly as it was a west coast site and the threat was seen as coming from the east. But it wasn't called Sellafield then, as the Ministry of Supply, to avoid confusion with their Springfields site near Preston, changed the name to Windscale after a small stretch of woodland on the banks of the River Calder called Windscale Nook.

Work began on two air-cooled reactors and by 1952 they were producing weapons-grade plutonium for the H-bombs. At that time the heat being generated was simply released up the stacks, so it was decided to build a civil nuclear power station to convert the heat into electricity — a peaceful use had been found for atomic energy.

But a year after it was opened by the Queen, a fire broke out in Pile No 1 and it all came close to being a total disaster. The temperature reached 1300° centigrade and some twenty thousand curies of radioactive iodine and other deadly isotopes were soaring up and out of the chimney. And yet people living in the area were not evacuated, even when the risky and perhaps panic-driven decision was taken to douse it with water. A mix of carbon monoxide and hydrogen might well have resulted in an explosion outdoing Chernobyl. It would be interesting to know if they had any emergency plans or if it were all *ad hoc*.

Days and weeks passed before it was decided to pour the locally produced milk away because of the radioactive Iodine. The dairy farmers demanded and received compensation for lost production and it is always said that during the time of the ban the milk yield mysteriously doubled.

A year later CND was formed.

Equally bad for the industry's image was the accidental discharge of radioactive effluent into the sea in 1985. This time the public were warned to keep away from a twenty-five mile stretch of beach and some parts were closed for six months — no help to the coastal tourist industry, who were not compensated.

There are so many complex issues surrounding Sellafield (it got its name back in 1981). As well as health and safety, there are environmental and economic issues, and political and social ones, not to mention moral. None of this though is surprising when you consider the size and complexity of the site. Within its two hundred and seventy-five hectares and four hundred buildings, there are two plutonium producing reactors, the world's first four nuclear reactors, a defunct Advanced Gas Cooled Reactor, (the giant golf ball) two nuclear reprocessing plants, Britain's main plutonium stockpile and vast areas devoted to the storage of high and intermediate level nuclear waste. Added to this is the economic factor that it provides employment for close on ten thousand Cumbrians.

I have often thought that this in itself is an added danger factor, as if you have ever found yourself driving over Corney Fell at shift-change time then the only safe thing to do is to get yourself into a lay-by as quickly as you can and cower there with your eyes shut while Cumbria's own equivalent of *The Whacky Races* roars past.

Conscious of the 'negative publicity' which the site had attracted, Sir Christopher Harding, the Chairman, put forward a plan to end the air of secrecy which had always surrounded it. If the public fully understood what went on there, he argued, they would loose their fear and drop their opposition. So, in 1982 an Exhibition Centre was opened. Little more than an Information Centre at first, its popularity grew to such an extent that in 1987 work began on the present Visitors Centre. Opened by the Duke of Edinburgh, it cost £5M, and visitor numbers rose to one hundred and fifty thousand a year.

1995 saw another change. Now the emphasis was less on information and more on 'education and entertainment'. Not, I think, a change for the better. I fully understand that after 9/11 it is no longer feasible to have conducted tours of the site, but was such dumbing-down necessary? The claim is that it is now aimed at fourteen year olds, but I would have thought it is more like ten. Lots of fun, lots of hand-on stuff and flashing lights, and plenty of 'historical' items such as a 1940's washing machine. There are some good jokes too: I liked the t-shirt with the two-headed sheep saying, 'I've been to Sellafield'. But when I was last there, the few grown-ups who had come in had a bemused look as they wandered slowly about and I fear that they left knowing little more than when they went in, which was probably precious little. It is understandable, but nevertheless a great pity that conducted tours are no longer possible. I was privileged, because of this book, to be taken on one and found it totally astonishing. You get no idea of the size of the place from the outside; it is like a small city and the inside of the Thermal Oxide Reprocessing Plant (THORP) is on a scale which is hard to grasp. Almost forty metres high and so full of pipes and cranes and galleries and deep dark storage tanks, it seemed at first like one of those places where the final scenes of a James Bond film are played out. But this wasn't fiction. It was hard commercial fact and I was so full of admiration for the people who could design and build such a thing. Inside the Thorp building there is a special public viewing platform and display charts on the walls showing clearly and exactly what is going on. And my guides explained that there really is no mystery to nuclear power. It is at its simplest just another way of producing steam to drive a turbine to produce electricity, but instead of fossil fuels being burned, the heat is generated by splitting uranium atoms. But as the public can no longer enter the site, I fear that the old aura of secrecy will surround the place again and that is not good for Sellafield or for the public.

The aim of the 'fun' in the Visitor Centre, as I see it, is to produce a generation which is not instinctively alarmed by the word *radioactive.* Understandable, but something of a struggle since 26th April 1986 when No 4 reactor at Chernobyl blew up and sent a radioactive cloud drifting over Europe, reaching Cumbria and coming down as rain, as if we haven't enough of the stuff ourselves. I am told that twenty-one years later two hundred thousand sheep in Cumbria are still declared unfit for human consumption, yet I am also told that a lamb chop from such a beast eaten every day for 12 months would be the equivalent dose of half a dental x-ray. What are we to believe? Have we become unnecessarily *radiophobic*?

It may be. Immediately after the Chernobyl explosion it was being claimed that nine thousand deaths could be expected. Some said hundreds of thousands. Clearly no one *knew*. Twenty years later and health statistics seem to show that only about fifty deaths can be directly related to it and most of those were among the heroic volunteers who went in to deal with it. And what is even more surprising — it certainly surprised the scientists who conducted the research — is that the wild life, the voles, mice, and such like, showed no signs of the genetic changes which had been expected, even though they had been exposed to the equivalent of eight thousand chest x-rays a day. Equally puzzling is the discovery that in America those states with the highest background radiation have the lowest incidence of cancer. Might it after all, as was once thought, be good for us in low doses? As yet we have no way of knowing, but I confess I still cannot look at the towers of Sellafield without something of a shudder and the fact is that it is not only the largest plutonium production and storage site, it is also the burial ground for nuclear waste of such toxicity that it will remain dangerous for hundreds of thousands of years. And it is that which seems so unacceptable. Leaving future generations to cope with a problem that we have left behind us.

* * *

Not many miles down the road from Sellafield is a legacy of a very different kind left to us by a previous generation: the Gosforth Cross.

I read somewhere once that Pope Gregory the Great advised the missionaries he sent out that if they came up against some well-established pagan cult or heathen religion, they should not try to stamp it out, but should be accommodating towards it and try to assimilate it in some way. And I am sure that they often did, just as I am sure that often enough their 'converts' held onto something of their old religion, *just in case*. It was only sensible. As I said, looking at the Dragon Stone at St Bees, you have to ask yourself whether it is St Michael, or is it perhaps Sigurd? Or could it possibly be both? In Gosforth Church it becomes quite clear what is going on.

A church of some sort — no more than a clay daubin building probably, strengthened with wattlework — may have been built by the Saxons on this site as early as AD 700 and it was still there a hundred years later when the Vikings came into the area, not to plunder and pillage as their ancestors had done, but to find somewhere they could settle after being driven out of Dublin. Then the Normans came shortly after 1100 and built a stone church, using as part of the foundation work some Viking hogback tombstones they found there. This in turn was replaced by a much larger Early English church in the thirteenth century, and then in 1789 there took place what has been described as a 'disastrous reconstruction' which obliterated what had stood for centuries. 'Improvements' continued and in 1896 dynamite was used to demolish the north end of the nave. It sounds like the grossest vandalism, but one beneficial result was that the blast revealed the hogback tombs which are now on display inside the church.

One is called *The Warrior's Tomb* and shows two armies facing each other with brandished swords and interlocking shields, but the leader of the army on the right is holding up a flag and the scene is thought to represent the truce between King Ethelred (the *Unready*, or rather *Ill-Advised*) and the Viking chief Grice, which took place at Hardnott in AD 1000 and which led to the humiliation of the English army. The Vikings had blockaded the harbour at Ravenglass and so prevented Ethelred's support troops from landing. Greatly outnumbered, he was obliged to surrender his standard, his troops to lay down their weapons and to march back bare-headed the way their had come.

The other tomb displays a different kind of battle: the slaying of the evil figure of the World Serpent, or perhaps (it is no longer clear) the Wolf Vidar at Ragnorak, the last great battle in the Norse sagas between the gods of Good and Evil. And at each end of the tomb is a 'crossless crucifixion', Christ with His arms outstretched — dying for us and overcoming evil. Two versions of the same story.

Moving along the north aisle we come to an archway in which there is an even more significant dualism: *The Fishing Stone*. Thought by some to have been part of a frieze in the pre-Norman church, this is a clear example of Norse mythology being used to illustrate a Christian theme. In the lower half we see a story any Viking would have been very familiar with. Thor, holding onto his famous hammer *Mjollnir*, has gone out fishing with the axe-wielding giant Hymir. Thor, having baited his line with the head of an ox, is trying to catch the evil World Serpent *Midgardsorm*. He did manage to catch it, but Hymir panicked when he

The Green Man

saw what was being hauled out of the waves and he cut the line, letting
the beast escape. So Thor failed, whereas in the upper half of the carving
we see a hart, a familiar Christian symbol, trampling on the same monster
and overcoming evil. Where Thor fails, so this sermon on stone says,
Christ is victorious.

On a capital only a few feet away from this is a carving of three
heads which, according to the guide book, are supposed to represent Past
Present and Future, but the luxuriant growth surrounding the one in the
middle and what looks like branches sprouting from his mouth suggests
to me that this might be a relic of a religion even older than either that of
the Norsemen or the Christians. He looks like *The Green Man* to me.

But outside the church stands what it is most famous for; the
Gosforth Cross. Fourteen feet high and more than a thousand years old,
it dates back to a time when the Nordic gods were beginning to fade
before the spread of Christianity, yet it features both.

The lower part is rounded like a tree trunk and represents Yggdrasil,
the ash tree whose roots and branches, according to Norse belief, support

the universe, binding together heaven, earth and hell. And on the top of the column is a Celtic cross, decorated with the triquatra, the triangular interlace pattern which signifies the Trinity.

The main shaft depicts many of the characters and events of *Ragnarok*, the Norse twilight of the gods, the ending of the world, when Good would finally be defeated by Evil, but when at the same time Evil would be overwhelmed by Good. For example, on the north side we see Odin doing battle with Surt, the fire giant, and with a winged dragon whose wings end, curiously in a triquatra. It is the east side though which is the most interesting. Starting from the top there is first of all a two-headed wolf/serpent, swallowing the sun with one head (a sign which heralded Ragnarok) while its other head is under attack from Odin's son Vidar. Then comes some interlace and below it we have a crucifixion scene, an image of the Centurion Longinus piercing Christ's side with a spear, and alongside Him is the Virgin Mary. Christian hope of eternal life overcoming scenes of Nordic despair.

It is quite amazing that the Gosforth Cross has survived all this time, survived the temptations of casual vandalism, and the even greater threat from the institutionalised vandalism of the Cromwellian era when even images of Christian saints, let alone pagan deities, were not to be tolerated and were knocked down from their niches and smashed to pieces.

Once however there were four such crosses. Two are quite lost, though small fragments of them are in the church, built into the same wall as the *Fishing Stone*. The fourth survived until 1789, when the Rector — let's name and shame the fellow — he was called (of all names) Charles Cobbe Church — cut it down to a height of four feet to make a sundial. Its truncated remains are now near the lych-gate, but it doesn't even have a sundial today. What can one say?

I can not leave Gosforth though without recording that on the road out of the village towards Santon Bridge is a place called Sorrowstones, where, I am told, criminals on their way to be hanged at Hanging How were given a last drink. Strangely needed, I've no doubt.

Eight

*Seascale. Grey Croft Stone Circle. Carl Crag and
Kokoarrah. Drigg. Ravenglass; the name. Agricola
and 20th Legion. The Fort and the Bath House.
Ravenglass Fair. William Stott. Pharaoh's Garage.
The village. The murder of Mary Bragg. Muncaster
Castle. Henry VI. Patrick Gordon-Duff-Pennington.
Thomas Skelton, the Fool of Muncaster. The Owl
Centre. The La'al Ratty.*

Time and again down the Cumberland coast you find towns which
claim to have been classy holiday resorts during the Victorian era and
later. Seascale is one of them, but I would take some convincing of that.
There is very little evidence of it apart from a massive parish church and

Above: Ravenglass - A steam train

nowadays it seems to be little more than a dormitory town for Sellafield workers.

The second half of its name comes from an Old Norse word *skali* meaning a wooden hut, so it was almost certainly one of the places the Vikings came to when they were driven out of Ireland and looking for somewhere to settle. But there were people here long before the Vikings, as the Grey Croft stone circle, almost right up against the Sellafield boundary, can be dated back to 2500 BC. We are lucky to have it at all, as it was considered a nuisance and ploughed under in 1820 and only restored by a Mr Fletcher and some boys from Pelham House School at Calderbridge in 1949. What a job they undertook. The circle is almost a hundred yards in diameter and there are ten stones, some nearly six feet high. While they were digging them out they also discovered some Bronze Age tools as well as flints and a Whitby jet ring.

The one other interesting thing in Seascale is only to be seen as you are driving out on the road towards Drigg and that is the oldest house in the town, Herding Neb Cottage. Once the only staircase it had was outside and people used to say of those who lived there that they were "forced to gang outside to go to bed." In its time it was a beer house, or *jerry-shop* as it was known locally and a popular meeting place for the local poaching fraternity. What makes it interesting now is a ship's figure head set into the wall. It is said to have been from a ship that was wrecked there in 1884 and to be a likeness of Lord Byron. It certainly looks like him, but a local historian has quibbled that the only wreck in that year was a Russian vessel carrying salt from Liverpool and it is hardly likely it would have had Byron at its prow. So the date is wrong. Byron was enough of a celebrity in his day to have been a figurehead and it would be mean to deprive Seascale of this tiny claim to fame.

To the north there is a hill which used to be known as Laking Hill — or Playing Hill — and until the mid nineteenth century it was a custom on the third Sunday in Lent for men and boys to play 'football' there. Not under FA Rules though. The aim was for one team to get the ball into the sea and for the other to get it up to where the golf course is now. Violence, seemingly, was not something they gave up for Lent.

There are two very curious rocks to be seen off the coast. One by the name of *Carl Crag,* and the story of that one is that the Devil was trying to build a bridge or causeway to the Isle of Man (we are not told why) and he was carrying a huge boulder in his apron (we are not told why he was wearing an apron either — it sounds so very domestic) but it slipped out and fell where we see it today, but the marks of his apron strings are still clearly to be seen in two white quartz stripes. The other rock is called *Kokoarrah*. Why? Well, Lewis Carroll is said to have visited the area, but I do know that that *Carreg* was the British/Celtic word for *rock* — hence *crag* — and that the Old Norse for *red* was *rauðr*, and as it is pronounced *Kokra*. the meaning might, prosaically, be *Red Rock*. It is sandstone after all and it is only the spelling that makes it look like an Australian bird reserve.

A little south of Seascale is the village of Drigg where Sellafield store their low level waste. It is all underground of course. Unlike the main site, there is nothing at all to be seen from the road and when the trees which have been planted around the perimeter fence have grown it will have all the look of a small forest. But at the end of the track that turns off by the Craft Shop — crammed with all the things you would expect in a craft shop and then so much more that you wouldn't, including excellent coffee — there is a wide expanse of beach and miles of sand dunes. It is just a shame that so many people drive down there to let their dogs run free, regardless of a notice asking them to keep them on a leash. Walking the dunes you wouldn't dare lift your eyes off the track for a moment for fear of being clarted with dog shit. At least the beach gets washed clean twice a day.

It is a great beach for sea birds, especially waders and I love those high piping calls the oystercatchers and redshanks make. And then there is the sound of the curlew telling you its name over and over again. It is such a melancholy sound, which is probably why it has attracted so many stories of ill-omen to itself. The Seven Whistlers for example. Six curlews are said to fly forever in search of their lost companion and when they are at last re-united the end of the world will come. Curiously, the godwit, a bird which looks very similar to the curlew, is taken to be a good omen and its name comes from two Old English words — *gōd* and *wiht* — meaning that it is a *good creature.* It would be nice to think that the tiny knot that you see scuttling in and out of the incoming waves breaking along the shore are named after King Canute, but apparently they aren't.

Folk-etymology, as my language tutor at university used to call it.

Only a few miles down the coast from Drigg is Ravenglass, but nowadays, if you want to get to Ravenglass the only sensible way of approach is from the south, down a narrow B road a mile or so north of Muncaster Castle and just where you come to that sudden 90° bend in the A595 as it crosses the River Mite and hares off in the direction of Holmrook. It is a bend so sudden and so severe that it could only be the work of civil engineers or bureaucrats; no normal traveller would ever have veered off quite so drunkenly. And in fact before macadam no normal traveller *could* have gone that way as the land is so flat and so low-lying that it would have been marsh and mud and that when it wasn't totally under water. What is now the B road must once have been the only safe route, keeping close to the coastline, even though it did mean crossing a ford at either end of the village. This was, we know, the route John Wesley took in 1759 on his way to preach to the people of Whitehaven, though he seems to have been none too pleased about being lied to about the safe-crossing times. "I have taken my leave of the sand road," he wrote in his journal, "especially as you have all the way to do with a generation of liars, who detain all strangers as long as they can, either for their own gain or their neighbours. I can advise no stranger to go this way." A little uncharitable of him, I think, not to say unchristian. They were just trying to earn a few extra coppers and after all, he did manage to make it to Whitehaven before nightfall and there are many worse places than Ravenglass to be delayed in.

The coastal route was also the way the Roman general Agricola took when he led the 20th Legion, *Valeria Victrix,* north from Chester in the spring of AD 79. (There is a statue of Agricola, I don't know why, over the entrance to Manchester Town Hall.) Tacitus, the historian, who was also Agricola's son-in-law, describes his progress as being through *aesturia ac silvas,* wooded estuaries, so presumably he came by way of the Mersey, the Lune, the Leven and the Duddon, eventually crossing the Esk by the ford at Waberthwaite. Even today, when you drive down that steep hill into Ravenglass for the first time, past the sandstone cottages and the elegant villas and then swing left under the railway bridge, nothing quite prepares you for the expanse of estuary you suddenly see spread out in front of you. If you are not prepared for it, and I certainly wasn't the first time I went, it is quite breath-taking. Agricola was probably less interested in its scenic than its strategic value. Even so, I imagine he could hardly have believed his eyes: an estuary big enough to safe-harbour the entire Roman fleet and with hills rising sharply behind it to form a first rate defensive position. It was there he built his fort. *Glanoventa* is the name we know it by — "the fort on the river bank". Logistically it could not have been better. He would not be so dependant on that tortuous overland route for supplies, and reinforcements could be on the scene very quickly indeed if they were ever needed. However, it would not, as they say, have been *all plain sailing.* In Conrad's *Heart of Darkness,* Marlow imagines a Roman commandant sailing up the Thames for the first time. "Sandbanks, marshes, forests, savages — precious little to eat fit for a civilised man, nothing but Thames water to drink. No Falerian wine… Here and there a military camp lost in the wilderness… cold, fog, tempests, disease, exile and death — death skulking in the air, in the water, in the bush." And it can't have been much different along the damp west coast of England.

The first fort he built would probably have been a somewhat provisional affair of turf and timber, just enough to give his troops some shelter from the wind and rain and snow of a Cumbrian winter. He would not have seen it as being permanent; he was keen to move on further to subdue the Picts. It was half a century later, when Hadrian was building the frontier wall, that Glanoventa was entirely rebuilt in granite, quarried from nearby Newton Knott. This new fort was a massive structure, two hundred yards square with walls up to five feet thick. Running water was piped in from a reservoir in the hills above it, and the living conditions, at least for the officers, bordered on the luxurious, as we can tell from what remains of their bath house — the tallest surviving Roman remains in the north of England. They had separate hot and cold baths, changing rooms and under-floor heating. Some of the hypocaust is still there and evidence has even been found of green glass in the windows and of rose-coloured plaster on the walls. It would be many centuries before England would see anything the likes of that again in its bathrooms.

But, as usual, the rank and file were seemingly not so spoiled. W.H. Auden gives us a shrewd guess as what it must have been like for them in his poem *Roman Wall Blues*

Over the heather the wet wind blows,
I've lice in my tunic and a cold in my nose.
The rain comes pattering out of the sky,
I'm a Wall soldier. and I don't know why.

And Tacitus records a mutiny in the "fort facing Ireland". Officers were murdered and the mutineers made their escape by sailing out to sea, but with the Roman Empire being what it was, it is hard to know where they thought they could escape to. Capture would have been quick, as no doubt was the punishment.

The last of the legions left Britain in AD 410, when Rome itself was under attack from the northern tribes and the forts and cities they had built, there being no longer any skilled masons to carry out repairs, would slowly have become dangerous ruins impossible to live in, and so as the years passed Glanoventa was abandoned and its name forgotten, but the Britons, who would have been working with and for the Romans, and had probably been living there long before the Romans arrived, stayed on in the area and when we next hear of it, the settlement has resumed its original Celtic name of Ravenglass: in Welsh (the nearest thing we have to that old language) *yr Afor Glas* means The Green River. It has nothing whatsoever to do with ravens or glass of course.

Other place names nearby tell of other settlers: the Angles and Saxons in *Irton* and *Santon,* and Vikings in *Waberthwaite* and *Murthwaite.* And then there were the Normans — parts of Muncaster parish church are thought to date back to the middle of the twelfth century. By 1208 Norman rule was fully established and Ravenglass was considered important enough for King John to grant Richard de Lucy, Earl of Egremont, a charter to hold a market every Saturday and an annual fair on St. James's Day, in payment for which he was to receive 'one gode palfrey' or saddle horse.

I suppose that when almost all your working hours and days were taken up in producing enough or earning enough simply to feed and house yourself and your family, fairs must have been something special. Life is immeasurably easier for us these days, but I do fear that in consequence we seem to have forfeited *special.* Entertainment has, for the most part, become something we sit passively in front of, not something we take part in, whereas the Ravenglass Fair involved everybody and by all accounts it sounds to have been a lot of fun.

It lasted three days and on the first morning all the Earl's tenants — it was part of their tenancy agreement — gathered on the common at Drigg on the Saltcoats side of the River Mite and marched in procession, no doubt to the accompaniment of drums, bugles and horns, over the ford and into the town where a proclamation was read out on the steps of the market cross and the Fair began. Livestock sales would have been the chief interest on the first day, but there was probably nothing you couldn't buy: poultry, butter and eggs, boots and bonnets, pots and pans from the travelling tinkers, ribbons for sweethearts and ballads too from the pedlars and packmen, and of course beer and in all likelihood, I shouldn't wonder, a little bit of nooky on the side as well.

It was also a sporting occasion. A poster for the 1829 Fair advertises a purse of five guineas for a race between cart horses. And there were boat races too, and a handsome belt and thirty shillings to be wrestled for and a hat to be run for.

But as the years passed the popularity and importance of the fair went into decline. The three days became one and eventually it faded altogether. The Saturday markets stopped and now even the market cross itself has gone. For seven hundred years it had stood there and generation after generation had sat and smoked and chatted on the steps around its base, until in the early 1900's they were dismantled — goodness knows why — and dumped onto the beach. There used to be a row of little terraced cottages called Gibraltar Row close to the shore and opposite what is now the Parish Hall, but they have gone too. But enough of the old Ravenglass still remains to make it one of the most endearingly curious little villages on the whole of the coast. And the Fair has been resurrected. It is not on 25th July, St James's Day, any longer. It is more likely to be a weekend nearer Midsummer's Day, or to coincide with the Three Peaks Yacht Race, but there are stalls on the village green, there is Morris dancing, people dress up in medieval costume and the ancient proclamation is read out. It may not be what it once was, but at least it exists.

On the green, with a fine view of the bay, and next to Rose Garth Guest House, where you can get really great crab sandwiches, there is The Holly House Hotel, which was once the studio home of the post-impressionist painter William Stott of Oldham, so called to distinguish him from another William Stott who is now even less well-known than the Oldham one! A painter of seascapes and of figures set in luxurious landscapes, he was a friend and admirer of Whistler. He must have been a close friend too as he painted a nude portrait of Whistler's mistress, Maud Franklin, which he called 'Venus Born of the Sea'. But they fell out when Whistler abandoned her. Stott bearded him in the Hogarth Club and called him "a liar and a coward." Whistler slapped his face and then, as he explained in a letter to the Club Secretary, "I administered a kick to that part of Mr Stott of Oldham's body that finally turned towards me, and that I leave him to specify." Stott was obliged to resign from the Club, but I think the moral victory was his. He died in 1900 when he was only 42, while on a sea voyage meant to be for his health.

One of the oldest buildings in Ravenglass is now the Post Office, on the right where the road narrows. Made of granite with walls almost three feet thick in places, it was almost certainly built from the stones of the Roman fort. Not nearly so old, but old enough to raise an eyebrow is the petrol pump outside what used to be Pharaoh's Garage. It still shows the price for when it was last used: 1/5d a gallon. That is about 7p in today's money and at today's prices might buy you just enough petrol to get you off the garage forecourt.

Continuing down the seaward side of the road is the Old Reading Room, which began as a chapel in 1865, but by the end of the century was a place where young men could gather to read in the Library, or to play darts or billiards. A little further down is a house now called *Cambria* which was the Poor House from about 1750 until 1839, its residents having to wear a yellow patch on their sleeve with the letters P (for pauper) and M (for parish of Muncaster) on it. No thought was given to their feelings in the matter.

To my mind, one of the curiosities of Ravenglass is that the houses on the seaward side of the road are all small and low and look very working-class. Whereas on the other side the houses are all far bigger, not grand but quite imposing. Did the two sides acknowledge each other? I suppose the difference comes from the grander ones being less liable to flooding. Today, working-class and humble-looking those seaward – facing houses may be, but they have the views and the sunsets and it is a quiet, pretty village, so a two-up, two-down terraced house there will cost you … well, you'll flinch when they tell you. .

When it was a thriving community it must have been far different and anything but quiet: four inns, eight provisions shops, three milliners, a baker, blacksmith, cobbler, ironmonger, joiner, laundry, slaughter house and a bank. The bank, now Heywood House, near where the market cross once stood, was a branch of the Cumberland Union Banking Company.

At the end of the street is Ship House, once The Ship Inn and run by William Wilson, a more genial man by all accounts than his elder brother who managed The Bay Horse immediately opposite. Did their clientele keep to their own side of the street? But when we come to the account of William's part in what became known as *The Battle of Annaside,* we will be left wondering what was meant by *genial,* and what sort of frivolity went on in The Bay Horse!

A flood gate was built at this southern end of the village after the disastrous flood of 1977, when there was three feet of water in many of the houses, much of it having come through the sewers and back up the lavatories, but when a combination of high winds and high tides is forecast you will still see people putting sandbags in their doorways. There is a price to be paid for living so close to the sea.

Ravenglass is quiet and genteel now, but once it was a busy port and not just in Roman times. In the sixteenth century it was home to a herring fleet. The herrings, it was said, "lye in sholes together so thicke in the sea at spawning, about August, as a ship cannot pass throw." Later its harbour was ideal for the smugglers' vessels bringing cheap tobacco, spirits and silk into the country from the Isle of Man. The black cattle of Ireland once landed there too. But the harbour began to silt up, and in 1914 the last tall ship came bringing in manure in the form of guano from South America for local farmers.

Opposite where the Bank used to be is Pennington House. Built in 1764 it is elegant home now, but with a sad story belonging to it. It is where poor Mary Bragg lived. So one story goes, she was a great beauty and two of the local young men both fell in love with her. Both proposed to her, but the losing suitor didn't take kindly to it. If he couldn't have her then no one would, and so he hired two ruffians to murder her. Her bloodstains, it is said, still appear on the doorstep to this day. A second

The price of petrol at Ravenglass.

version tells a very different story though. According to this one, she fell in love with a footman at Muncaster House, and this so angered one of the housemaids there, who was also in love with him, that she it was who hired a pair of ruffians. They called at Mary's house telling her that her lover was seriously ill and was asking to see her. Off she went with them, but she never reached Muncaster House. They killed her and threw her body in the river, where it wasn't found for several days, by which time, it's said, eels had eaten so much of it that the Coroner could not say how she died.

Good stories, both of them. Unfortunately, details of the inquest and the witness statements are still in the Whitehaven Records Office and there is also a report in the *Cumberland Pacquet* telling its readers that "there did not appear a single circumstance to warrant an opinion of violence or cruelty having been committed upon the body, but there were strong reasons for suspecting that the death of the unfortunate girl had been her own rash act." The verdict was "found drowned".

And yet…her father, Henry Bragg, is recorded as saying at the inquest "that he believes verily and truly that Sarah Jackson of Muncaster House and John Pickthall of the same place can give material information and are necessary witnesses." But seemingly they were never called. Was John Pickthall a footman at Muncaster House, and was Sarah a housemaid? Maybe there is some truth in the second version. Did the people in the big house look after their own? Whatever the truth, the "unfortunate girl" came to an unhappy end.

Coming back to the beginning of the street and opposite the Post Office is the *Pennington Arms Hotel,* once *The King's Arms* where coach horses use to be exchanged. It closed in 1996, but is being re-opened by the Pennington family. And rightly so, as their *Wild Cat* coat of arms has always been up there on the wall.

Originally from the Furness Peninsular, where a small village not far from Ulverston still bears their name, the Penningtons can trace their roots back further than many another aristocratic family in the country. Land was granted by the Lord of Egremont to Alan de Penitone in 1208 and by 1248 a castle had been built there by Gamel de Mulcastre, sometimes written as Moelcastre. A *mole,* from the Latin *moles*, meaning a great mass of something, developed to mean a breakwater built out to sea to protect a harbour, so Mulcaster (as it was first called) was a castle on a promontory by the sea. Approaching it from the gateway on the A595 today we don't realise that until we have walked up the long drive and gone behind the main building. It is only then that you see what a spectacular and commanding view it has over the Esk Valley.

1462 is an important date in the family's history, as it was then, so the story goes, that two of the Muncaster estate's shepherds came across a bedraggled and exhausted stranger who asked them the way to the Castle. As we are advised in the Bible, "Be not forgetful to entertain strangers, for thereby some have entertained angels unaware." This was not an angel, but he was their King, Henry VI, escaping from his defeat at the Battle of Hexham. Sir John Pennington entertained him for several days, before he set out again, only to be betrayed by a monk, taken prisoner and finally executed in The Tower. But before he left Mulcaster he gave his host a glass bowl and declared that the Penningtons would

The Henry VI Tower at Muncaster

enjoy good fortune as long as the bowl remained unbroken. It became known as 'The Luck of Mulcaster' and is still intact, but, wisely, is not on show. There is a 'Luck of Workington' and another, I believe, at Levens. The area is wick with them.

I prefaced this account with the words *so the story goes* as there is, sadly, no firm historical evidence to back it up. If there were, then it would be mentioned in Ralph Griffiths monumental biography of the king, but I am afraid there isn't. But as his whereabouts after Hexham do seem to be uncertain, one cannot be sure that it isn't true. All the same, if you take the path opposite the entrance to the Castle Garden Centre it brings you to Chapels Monument, commemorating the spot where the King was *found*. It is, perhaps appropriately, a kind of folly — a grey stone tower which looks as if it once had a Gothic church attached to it. Not that it ever did. It was erected there by the first Lord Muncaster about the year 1800, yet looks far more ancient, which of course it is meant to do.

Another sad fact is that the Lords of the Manor were not always as kind to their tenants as Sir John was to that possibly fictitious and woebegone wanderer. Writing in her book *Ravenglass Through the Ages* Barbara Newton tells of the Mulcaster Manor Court which was held twice a year, at Pentecost and at Martinmass, when not only did the rents become due but other oddities had to be paid to the Estates Steward. For instance there was a form of Death Duty: twenty pennies to be paid if a tenant died, on top of which was the widow faced the payment of a 'herriot', which was not a Yorkshire vet but another feudal tax, whereby if the deceased had rented, say, a farm and two other fields then his Lordship was entitled to *three* of the most valuable beasts – horses or cows – that the widow had inherited. He was also entitled to 'boons' – days when his tenants were obliged to work for him, digging peat, harrowing, shearing for example, without any payment. On and on these dues went. One penny halfpenny for every calf born on his estate, twopence for a foal, even a penny for a swarm of bees. At Eastertide his grateful tenements had to present him with eggs. There is no mention of *droit de seigneur* though, I am glad to say.

The first Lord Muncaster, the one who built the Chapels Monument, seems to have been a restless, hot-tempered individual. He dabbled in politics but didn't get far, even though he was a friend of Pitt. He tried the army, but that didn't suit him either. Eventually his father, who was living on one of his estates in Yorkshire, pulled some strings, called in a few debts which helped him to a vacancy in the Irish peerage and so the fifth baronet became the first Lord Muncaster but without a seat in the House of Lords.

Muncaster Castle

What he did settle down to was the renovation of the Castle, using the original fortress tower as one corner, he built the elegant rectangular building we see today. He started the library and it was he who created the shrubbery and who planted most of the hardwood trees which still grace the estate today. To his credit he was also passionately opposed to the slave trade and was among those who introduced the Bill into the House of Commons to abolish it.

But for all the good he did, his life was marked by tragedies. His only son died at the age of eight. His wife Penelope — 'One of the best of wives', as her memorial says in Muncaster Church — was killed in a riding accident. Five years later his eldest daughter died. He lived on to be 76 and died without an heir, so the title and the estate went to his brother, General Lowther Pennington. He must have been another hot-head as he once killed a man in a duel, having called him out for a 'foolish quarrel about humming a tune.'

His grandson, General Augustus, the Fourth Lord Muncaster, carried out even grander work on the house, covering and converting the courtyard into a splendid dining room. The Fifth and last Lord Muncaster died in 1917 and the estate went to his mother's family, the Ramsdens. It was they who first opened the grounds to the public and created an animal park. In 1983 Sir William Pennington-Ramsden handed it over to his daughter, the present owner, Mrs Gordon-Duff-Pennington.

When you go to Muncaster Castle, if you are lucky, you may meet Patrick Gordon-Duff-Pennington. I was going to say that he is 'larger than life' but that is such a terrible cliché. No one is larger than life – except for Patrick, who is larger than life and who is also the author of the most anarchic book of memoirs ever written, *Those Blue Remembered Hills.* It does begin at the beginning, but you don't even get to the foot of the first page before the digressions start. He explains that at his Christening he had "a generous endowment of four godparents. Two were never heard of again; one died who had a sister, an eminent historian with whiskers on her chin; and the fourth gave a devastating demonstration of a Sportsman's Advice to his Son by not taking the cartridges from his gun when he shot off his toe crossing a fence near Peebles in 1931". Interspersed with some of his own sparkling and rumbustious poems, the book is full of snippets that nothing prepares you for. "While nanny slept, guinea pig on knee, the fascinated children watched it reproduce and eat the babies one by one — a better biology lesson than Wetty Morris' lectures on the birds and bees at Eton."

He is a very blunt man and means every word of it when he says that he wants the house to be seen as "an integral part of the life of the Western Lake District, and not as an isolated enclave within less privileged surroundings." And also when he concludes the Guide Book with the words, "It is your inheritance as well as ours."

That Patrick wrote the Guide Book himself is clear from the second paragraph. Who else, referring to a portrait in the Library of his father-in-law aged nine, would have added, "He came second in the Grand National in 1927 on Bovril III, a horse with one eye." Or that in the Great Hall he is particularly attached to a vast table "which the experts allege is a fake."

There is no point in my trying to describe the beauty of the rooms in Muncaster Castle. I couldn't do it. The Library alone is sumptuous —

octagonal in shape and with more than 6,000 books which I wasn't allowed to touch.

There is one thing that I do have to take issue with though. At the end of a passageway on the first floor is the famous portrait of Thomas Skelton, the sixteenth century Fool of Muncaster, in full-length motley and accompanied by his 'will', a scroll half as long as himself. Now Patrick claims that it was Thomas Skelton who gave the word 'tomfoolery' to the language and that Shakespeare used him as the model for his character in *King Lear*. Sorry, Patrick, it won't do. Just as with the story of Henry VI, people at Muncaster again seem to have been a little *inventive* with their history. The Oxford English Dictionary records the first use of 'tomfool' as 1356 and the character in *Lear* who says 'Tom's a cold" is neither jester nor madman. He is Edgar, the Duke of Gloucester's son, who disguises himself as a 'bedlam beggar' to escape the murderous intentions of his illegitimate brother Edmund. But, be those boring facts as they may, the story has prompted Jennings Brewery to create a *Tom Fool* beer and to sponsor a Feast of Fools when members of the National Guild of Jesters (and no, that is not a joke) compete for the title of *Fool of Muncaster*.

Fool of Muncaster Thomas Skelton may have been, but he had an odd, not to say cruel sense of humour. A story goes that Helwise, the daughter of Sir Allan Pennington, was plighted to marry Sir Ferdinand Huddleston of Millom Castle, but she had fallen in love with a carpenter on the Muncaster estate, Will of Whitbeck. So Sir Ferdinand persuaded Thomas to kill him. Thomas had a grudge against the carpenter and gladly chopped off his head while he was asleep, then bounced into the Castle announcing, "I have hid his head under a heap of shavings and he will not find it so easily when he awakes." His ghostly presence is said to be felt in the Tapestry Room. I would not care to meet up with him. Another curious thing is that since the portrait was cleaned in 1982 the will can now be read and it seems to suggest that he lived in Wigan. Now that must be a joke.

The castle Gardens are a joy in themselves all year, but especially in the spring when rhododendrons are in flower. And since 1987 there is also an Owl Centre, which its founder, Tony Warburton insists is not an owl zoo, but rather a 'Noah's Ark' for owls, where local wildlife casualties

The Owl Centre, Muncaster.

are treated and returned to the wild and where owls facing extinction in their own countries are bred to 'buy time' in the hope that conditions in the wild may improve so the birds can be returned. I can't help thinking that in most cases this is to be romantically optimistic. Will things improve? Could birds bred in cages generation after generation know how to live outside them? They have had some success, breeding and returning pairs of the mighty European Eagle owl to parts of Sweden. And in this country they have released almost 1500 barn owls which were bred in Muncaster. It may not be a zoo, but it is a privilege to be able to see the magnificent Great Grey Owl and the tiny Pygmy Owl and the odder ones such as the Brown Fish Owl and the very rare Burrowing Owl.

Muncaster is now one of Cumberland's major tourist attractions and of course to enthusiasts the world over, the name of Ravenglass means one thing first and foremost and that is the *La'al Ratty* the little narrow-gauge railway which hauls coach loads of visitors the seven miles from Ravenglass up through the Miterdale and Eskdale as far as Boot and Dalegarth. The *La'al Ratty,* or Ravenglass and Eskdale Railway, to give it its proper name, owes its beginning not to tourists though, but like so much of the history of the county, to haematite. In 1871 the Whitehaven Iron Mines Company opened a mine at Boot in Eskdale and decided that instead of shifting their ore to the coast by cumbersome horse and cart as was the normal way, it would be more efficient and more in keeping with the go-ahead spirit of the times to build a railway of their own that would join up with the Furness Railway at Ravenglass and so on to the expanding town of Barrow in Furness. Opened in 1875 with a three feet gauge, it was so successful that within a year it was carrying passengers as well, then freight and before long that new breed of people called tourists. The changes it made to the daily life of the local communities must have been enormous and all went well for more than a quarter of a century until some busybody wrote to the government complaining about the dangerous state of the track. The then President of the Board of Trade, one Winston Churchill, ordered an inspection and the line was promptly closed down in 1908. One thinks of the years of the Great War as being years of misery and austerity, but rich eccentrics could still afford to play and one such, the model maker Wenman Basset-Lowke who had been running a miniature railway in his garden at Irton Hall, decided that the old Eskdale line could provide him and his friends with even more fun. The three foot gauge was ripped up and re-laid as fifteen inches and by Easter 1916 there were daily trains running as far as Eskdale Green sometimes carrying as many as four hundred passengers and more a day at the height of the summer season. It was closed down during the Second World War and although 1946 saw its re-opening, its future looked increasingly uncertain until a group of enthusiasts raised enough money to buy it and now the *La'al Ratty* is flourishing once again. *La'al Ratty*? There is more than one theory to explain the origin of that name, but I doubt if you have to look any further than the name of the contractor who built the first line back in 1874. He was a Mr Ratcliffe and what other nickname could he have expected his navvies to give him? It was probably Little Ratty's Railway from the very start.

There is a splendid little book called *Ravenglass: Roman Port to Railway Junction* by Peter van Zeller, one of the regular train drivers, and he kindly invited me to join him for a journey on the footplate. It was a dullish Friday morning in mid October when I went, but even so there were plenty of passengers waiting to get on. There really is something special about steam trains. I have noticed that they always seem to make people smile. And it's not just old folks remembering their summer holidays by the seaside; children are just as excited. Everyone at Ravenglass station wanted a photograph and the guard — a man clearly in his seventies — told them where best to stand and they all did as they were told. And I was in all their photographs as *I* was with the driver. I could feel their envy. Quite right too.

It was thirty-five years ago that Peter van Zeller came to Ravenglass and thought he might give train driving a go for a couple of years and you can tell that he still doesn't really look at it as being a job of work. It is a passion. It's a love affair. You only have to watch him polishing the brass work and oiling whatever it was he was oiling. There always has been something sexual about steam trains — all those pistons and thoughts of *Brief Encounter.*

Off we went "shuffling gouts of steam" as Philip Larkin put it. And dropping sand on the rails as it was a damp day. Leaves on the line is not a joke, Peter assured me. Steam trains have that wonderful smell and those sounds. And I was allowed to pull the chain that sounded the whistle whenever we came to a farm crossing. The only drawback was that with two of us on the footplate there wasn't a lot of room to spare and whenever Peter shovelled coal into the firebox, with a sort of long-handled kitchen shovel, blobs of jet black water splashed down on my trousers. "It's clean dirt is that though," he said. "It'll wash out." And it did.

We were soon reaching speeds of over fifteen miles an hour and easily overtook a hen pheasant which tried to keep up with us. And we scared all the sheep, sent them running away frantically and we scared them again on the return trip. Short memories they seem to have, do sheep.

Although it is small, it would be a mistake to think of the La'al Ratty as being some kind of toy. It isn't. For one thing, safety is taken very seriously. Peter was in regular radio contact with the man back in the signal box, telling him where we were, the state of the track and so on. But the passengers' attitude seems to be far more casual. As we approached the next to last station, *Muncaster Mill,* there was a young woman standing on the platform taking a photograph of us. "Does she want me to stop I wonder?" said Peter. And as we drew slowly alongside her, she lowered her camera, looked us in the eyes and nodded. She did.

It was a great journey. You get a totally new perspective. It's not like driving on the roads and it's not like walking. You are somehow *in* this landscape. Two hours passed so quickly and as I blew the whistle for the last time as we inched carefully into the station at Ravenglass there were more people waiting there on the platform. And they were all smiling.

Although the railways brought the tourists, and although it is the *La'al Ratty* that has made the name of Ravenglass so widely known, if you were to ask any archaeologist they'd say that the whole enterprise had been a complete disaster, particularly the main Whitehaven to Ravenglass line which smashed its way through the ancient sites, destroying the medieval saltpans near Brighouse Farm and, which is far worse of course, obliterating for all time whole tracts of the Roman Fort. But I suppose if you asked the average tourist which they would prefer – a Roman Fort or the *La'al Ratty* – there'd be no contest.

Nine:

*Eskmeals. The Nature Reserve. Natterjack toads.
The Firing Range. QinetiQ. Waberthwaite. Richard
Woodall. Hams and sausages. Bill Knowles and
Cumberland and Westmorland Wrestling. The Battle
of Annaside. Beachcombing. A message in a bottle.*

South of Ravenglass, where the River Esk does a surprising twist to
head back north on itself again, there is a stretch of sand dunes which are
marked on the Ordnance Survey map in large red letters as a DANGER
AREA. This is the Eskmeals Firing Range, where limiting public access
has had the advantage of allowing the area to go very much its own way
and now it is also a Nature Reserve stretching out over some 160 acres.

As the winds blow in from the Irish Sea and shift the sands about,
so you might, if you are lucky, come across a Roman coin, or, even older,

Above: Waberthwaite - the home of the sausage

162

a piece of worked flint. The stone axe heads roughed out in the Langdales at sites such as Harrison Stickle were brought down here to the coast to be worked on, smoothed and polished. You might also see one of our rarest amphibians, the natterjack toad, but as they are mostly nocturnal that would be very lucky, and even if one did happen to out in daylight they are very skilled at camouflage, and can lighten or darken the colour of their skin to blend in with the colour of the sand around them. What does make them different from the common toad is the yellow band running down their backs, and that having such short legs they are more adept at running than hopping or jumping. Another odd feature is that they are not very good swimmers and have even been known to drown. You may not see one, but there is every chance that you might hear them, as they are the noisiest amphibian we have and when they come out of hibernation in March and the breeding season starts the sound of their croaking can be heard up to a mile away, which is not so surprising as the throat gland they puff up when they do so can be even bigger than their heads. But I don't believe that the sound that they make has given them their name, even though my dictionary suggests that it has. *Jack* is a generic name given to a male, as in *jackdaw* or *jacksnipe,* so that presents no problem but the full name *natterjack* predates the verb *to natter* so that rules that bit out. I can never resist a linguistic challenge, and this one surrendered pretty quickly. The snake we call an *adder* was once known as a *nœdre* and an orange was once a *norange* (yes, think of the Spanish *naranja*) so what if this toad was once an *atterjack*? And I think it was. *Atter* is an obsolete word for venom and though toads are not venomous, they are so ugly and warty (and this one has that yellow stripe too) that people have often thought they were. In *As You Like It*, Shakespeare, who is usually a good naturalist, calls toads 'ugly and venomous'.

But if the toads are not venomous, there are some poisonous plants growing among these dunes. The yellow flowers of the ragwort are common enough everywhere, but its leaves are rich in an alkaloid poison and birds have learned to avoid those orange and black caterpillars of the cinnabar moth that we see feeding on them, and anyone who owns a horse will know how deadly they can be; it really doesn't take very much ragwort to infect the animal's liver. And in the valleys between the dunes you will find henbane, which gives us hyoscine. In small doses hyoscine is a sedative and can be given to alleviate sea-sickness, but it was a far larger dose that the famous Dr Crippen gave his wife. It's ironic really that he then tried to get away by sailing across the Atlantic, but his queasiest moment must without doubt have been when he found the American police were waiting for him on the dockside at New York.

There are some plants there that are good for us though. Heartsease for one. The old herbalists believed that an infusion of it would mend a broken heart, and sea holly is not only one of the most beautiful blues that there is, its root used to be candied and sold as 'eryngoes', an aphrodisiac for the elderly, or as Gerard tactfully puts it, "for restoring the aged and amending the defects of nature in the younger."

Normally, it would have to be said, walking along sand dunes you don't get much of a view, sea on one side, dunes on the other, but here the Drigg and the Eskmeals dunes have folded themselves back around the bay like a crab's claws so you are able to look back at Ravenglass with its houses so tiny they might be toys, and behind them, ringing it like an amphitheatre, there is the huge panorama of the high fells. It could not be more dramatic.

A mile or so down the backroad from the Reserve, going towards Bootle Station, there is drama of a very different kind. First you notice the CCTV cameras keeping watch in both directions, and then you come to the Firing Range, which is owned by the Ministry of Defence but operated by a company called QinetiQ. (It is pronounced *Kinetic* and is one of those silly pseudo-phonetic names which are meant to be eye-catching. This one though is not only silly, it is a swine to type.) It is a commercial company formed in 2001 from the MOD's Defence Evaluation and Research Agency, but the history of the Eskmeals range goes much further back than that, and Skelda Hill which has given its name to one of their batteries suggests a Viking settlement. But it first opened as a firing range in the 1890's and was an early testing site for the guns made by Vickers in Barrow-in-Furness. The present company has some great photographs of those times on its walls. In one, taken in the 1920's, the officials (dignitaries, scientists, engineers? Impossible to tell) are resplendent in bowler hats and riding boots and look very self-important.

With the outbreak of war, all that changed. The military arrived and the site housed some four hundred members of the Royal Artillery. They must have been hectic days. Eight million shells are estimated to have been fired into the Irish Sea last century and I imagine that the majority of them fell in those six years. It was such a sensitive area that it is only recently that the range has appeared on Ordnance Survey maps.

The army has gone now and the number of employees is down to eighty, but these are specialists. I was taken to see the site of the AS90, a 155mm self-propelled howitzer which is being upgraded. The technology, which is probably bewildering, is also invisible. Alongside it was a mobile radar tracking device — all shiny white and looking as innocuous as any burgher van — but with over a million pounds worth of equipment inside it. Mostly the ammunition which is fired from it is inert as it is the system which is being tested, not the shells. Nevertheless, no one is ever near it when it is fired. The engineers measuring the shell's velocity etc. are all safely inside reinforced concrete buildings. A shell from an AS90 can reach almost thirty kilometres, which is not all that far from the Isle of Man, so there is an exclusion zone going out as far as fifty kilometres and covering an area from St Bees to Millom and upwards for a height of eighty thousand feet. Shells have to go high if they are to get the distance, and in the 1950's the Blue Water rockets were tested here.

There has never been an accident at Eskmeals and they do not intend to have one. Safety probably occupies more time than firing. In the Control Centre there are screens for each of the CCTV cameras and a radar screen covering the whole area. Every battery is in constant contact with the Centre and if anything untoward should happen then all activity is stopped instantly. And, as 'untoward' can include summer tourists sailing blithely down the coast, there is a vessel on stand-by at Whitehaven to escort them politely to safety.

Eskmeals is an obvious place for a firing range. It is remote. The noise is not going to disturb many people. And there is a huge expanse of water to be fired into. The present site covers over fourteen hundred acres, yet comparatively little is in actual use. No tanks trundle about ripping up the land, so it has become an extension to the Nature Reserve, with three Sites of Special Scientific Interest within its fences. It has even become home to a herd of about fifty roe deer which seem to have wandered from Muncaster. Timid though they are, the noise does not seem to bother them.

It was the first day of spring when I was there. Sunshine, a cloudless blue sky and a smattering of snow on the hills. It looked idyllic. And the people who had shown me round had been so kind and so helpful that I was almost at Bootle railway station before my mind caught up with itself and I remembered that the ultimate purpose of it all is death and destruction. But that is, as they say, *the world we live in.* The way we used to live was evident from a truly impressive building opposite the station, bearing letters which read *The Lancashire Banking Company* and dated 1902. It was big enough to have employed a few dozen people by the look of it and many of them would have been called *clerks.* A word that begins to sound so strange. No one is a clerk today.

Turning back on yourself at Bootle and heading north again (and you should) you come to Waberthwaite. Waberthwaite may be one of the tiniest hamlets in the whole of the Lake District, but its funny-sounding name is famous throughout the country, let alone the county, thanks to Richard Woodall and the Waberthwaite sausage. From the outside, the shop, which doubles as the village Post Office, looks decidedly quaint, and stepping inside is like stepping back into another age. Most of the original Victorian shop fittings are still there, but not because the Woodalls can't be bothered to bring themselves up to date; this frontage is deliberate. It points to a long family tradition and to traditional ways of producing a high quality product. Nothing quite prepares you for what you find if you are taken through a plain wooden door in a far corner of the shop. It is like entering Dr Who's *Tardis.* You walk into a vast and complex series of spotless and gleaming rooms, none of which can be seen from the street outside, and there you find a staff of thirty people producing the sausages, the ham and the bacon which go on sale not only in Cumbria, but in Fortnum and Masons and in Harrods, and which are brought to the Queen's table in Balmoral Castle.

The family tradition goes back to 1828, when Hannah Woodall's husband died suddenly leaving her with five children to bring up at a time when there was no form of social security. Many a rural family in those days had their own pig and Hannah, with the help of her eldest son, Jackson, thought to make a little extra money by offering to do the curing for them. The offer was gladly accepted by more and more people and before long it had grown into a business, and today it is being run by the 7th and 8th generations of that same family.

The most senior member of the family today is Richard Barnes Woodall — known everywhere as *Bar* — and whom I had first met in his capacity as President of Whitehaven Rugby League Club. At home in Waberthwaite he made me tea and told me of his hands-on beginning in the business. At the age of fifteen he was given the job of killing the pigs. It was always done on a Saturday, he said, though he didn't know why. It just was. And he would go to the farm, the smallholding or cottage, wherever it was where there was a pig to be killed. What he remembers is that no one ever wanted to see their pig actually being killed. They seemed genuinely fond of them and as soon as he had his humane killer in his hand he was by himself, but once the job was done they were back again and willing to help with slitting the beast's throat and hang it up to collect the blood for black puddings. The real skill then, he told me, was cutting it cleanly in half with a cleaver. There was some pride to be felt in a precise, neat cut. Next it would be scalded and cleaned and on Sunday he would go back to cut it up, cutting out the hams joints, the belly for bacon and so on. Then came the curing. He went on with this job until he was married. It wasn't that his wife June objected to the killing, but they wanted weekends to themselves and killing was a Saturday job.

Most of the pork imported into this country today is from animals which have been kept in cramped conditions, sometimes in what are little more than crates, but Woodalls manage their own herd of 180 breeding sows which are housed in straw-filled barns with natural light and fresh air and with a large outdoor area they can move about in. There are no growth promoters or hormones added to their feed either and they are not injected with brine. The curing process is totally traditional: salt, brown sugar and saltpetre is rubbed into the meat by hand and it is then laid on a bed of salt for a month, after which the joints are washed and allowed to mature, some for as long as twelve months. It was Woodalls' ham that was on the menu of the Titanic and Woodalls' sausages used to be served on Concorde.

It was the growth of the supermarkets which led to their expansion and success in the 1960's. They had been content in the post-war years to be small-scale grocers, but this new competition meant they either had to change or they would go under as many another village shop did. The change they decided on was to offer their customers a product whose quality might just possibly be matched, but could not be bettered, and this was the goal Richard Woodall set himself, and which he set himself in what was and still is a tiny hamlet on the Cumbrian coast. The idea itself was bold enough; the achievement is astonishing. And recognition of their achievement came in 1990 when they were awarded a "Royal Warrant". Now on the wall of the shop is the Royal Coat of Arms and the words "By Appointment to H.M. Queen Elizabeth II, Suppliers of Traditional Cumberland Sausage, Cumberland Ham and Bacon".

It is the sausage which is my favourite and this might be because of its *secret ingredients.* Spices were imported into Whitehaven in the eighteenth century and they have long been included along with the 95% meat. The actual ingredients may not be a *real* secret, but the combination and the quantities are; they are known only to Richard himself and to one other member of the family. The recipe for it is in safe keeping in the bank, and he isn't even saying which bank.

Directly across the road from Woodalls' shop lives Bill Knowles, whose family has also distinguished itself: as Cumberland and Westmorland wrestlers. And looking at the number of silver cups in Bill's sitting room — and these were the ones they could keep; the ones they won outright — they must have been formidable opponents. He himself was the twelve stone world champion in 1953 and 1954, but he was never as good as his father, he says, yet when I asked him if it was his father who had taught him and trained him, he looked puzzled. No, it was something you just picked up as a kid and he had begun wrestling with his mates in the school yard and in the fields after school around Bootle. It was a bad accident to his knee in the Egremont Crab Fair when he was twenty-six that brought an end to his active wrestling career, but with all his skill and experience he was invited to become a judge, something he is always glad to do as clearly the comradeship is one of the things about the sport that he seems to value most.

The rules of Cumberland and Westmorland Wrestling could not be simpler. The contestants stand chest to chest, and when told to *tek hold* they grasp each other round the body and the first one breaking his hold or touching the ground with any part of his body except his feet looses the bout. If they should both fall over at the same time it's called a *dogfall* and doesn't count. So, if it's all so simple, what's the attraction? Well, it's not like Sumo, Bill says, not just two big blokes shoving each other about; there's craft and skill in it, but as the Scot, Rob McNamara, who won the All Weights World Championship for ten successive years, weighs twenty-four stone, size must matter. There are two other things in the sport's favour though I think: the costume and the long tradition.

The Icelandic sagas record that a wrestling ring was a permanent feature of their annual parliament – the *althing.* And their wrestling style, called *Hryggspena,* was very similar to Cumberland and Westmorland, but there is no clear evidence that the Vikings brought it here. It seems likely however, as there is a bout depicted on a ninth century Celtic Cross on Eilean Mor in the Sound of Jura. Curiously there is also one to be seen on a 1380 misericord in Chester Cathedral. The earliest written reference we have comes from 1656, when the Associated Ministers and Churches of the Counties of Cumberland and Westmorland (a bunch of Puritan kill-joys if ever there was) decreed that "All scandalous persons hereafter mentioned are to be suspended from the Sacrament of the Lord's Supper: any person that shall upon the Lord's Day play at dice, cards, football, wrestling…" And on and on the list of offences goes.

The sport's distinctive costume – the white Long Johns, socks and embroidered knickers – are part of the attraction, certainly for the cameras of the tourists. The reason for it is that it is a working man's sport, and when they took off their shirts and breeches that's all they had "their drawers and flannel waistcoats" as Dickens observed when he watched an event. The embroidery came into fashion, and no one seems to know exactly why, in the 1860's.

It was a sport that has drawn big crowds in its time: twelve thousand spectators are reckoned to have gathered on the Carlisle racecourse in 1811. But sometimes the bouts weren't all they seemed. There was a good deal of money to be won and there must have been gambling involved as well, as some matches were suspected to have been rigged, " barneying", it was called and so a governing body was set up in 1906 to regulate affairs.

In more recent years, they in turn have set up Wrestling Academies to teach the youngsters and to keep the tradition alive. Waberthwaite's own Academy probably first began in the early 1900's and has had its good and not-so-good times, but it was re-formed in 1991 and looks to be flourishing now under Tom Porter, Bill's nephew. He has some twenty-five wrestlers in training there, coming from a wide area, from Gosforth as far south as Broughton. Aged between seven and twenty-five, and with a few girls in the Academy too, they have had their successes, winning the Academy Shield in 1998 and again in 2000. The wrestling is as popular as ever among spectators, but the problem is getting the wrestlers. Tom has been going to local schools and showing them the basics, but even then when you've got them interested, there can be a problem persuading some of them to wear the traditional embroidered bit. It seems it can be a bit embarrassing these days.

This is a very quiet stretch of coast, but it hasn't always been so. On 21st August 1838 the *Cumberland Pacquet* ran a headline *"The Battle of Annaside!"* The villain who was responsible for it was William Wilson, the landlord of the Bay Horse Inn at Ravenglass. He had been earning a tidy sum on the side by selling cobbles from the beach, probably for use as ships' ballast. And he had taken so many from Annaside that the sea began coming in so far that roads and even house were washed away. He was asked to stop, but as the newspaper put it, he carried on "totally regardless of the injury that he was doing by persevering in such a practice; and what was worse, on his part, he treated with great insolence and contempt the expostulations and reasonings of those whom he was injuring by his conduct, thus, as it were, adding insult to injury." The inhabitants, we are told, "at first mildly attempted to expostulate with him", but eventually they had had enough of expostulation and on 17th August when three of Wilson's ships arrived and began to fill their holds again they pelted the crews with stones and forced them to retreat on board. But back at Ravenglass, Wilson reacted by gathering together added supporters, bribed with some free ale probably, and they sailed in force into Annaside again the following morning. They were armed with bludgeons and Wilson himself, a massive figure of a man apparently, was wielding a metal pump handle. But the villagers were ready for them and were backed by reinforcements from Whitbeck and Bootle. By all accounts it was a bloody battle and though no one was actually killed there were some serious injuries on both sides. But the Annaside men were fiercely supported by their womenfolk who were hurling stones and abuse and adding to the general mayhem. It was only when Wilson himself went down with a fractured skull that the Ravenglass men picked him up from the beach and ran back to their ships. The battle was over. Reading the report, it is clearly the behaviour of the women that caught the paper's attention most. "The language of the females, we are told, was of a most disgusting and revolting description, and shocked every one who heard them. They would, our informant observes, all have been much better employed had they been at home mending their stockings." I bet the *informant* would not have dared tell them that to their faces.

Pebble beaches can be some of the best to walk along. Not that they make for easy walking; they don't. If you are not careful you can twist an ankle in no time. But they are by far the most interesting. And it's not only the things that get caught up among the stones, it's the stones themselves. Most of those along our beaches simply come in various shades of grey, the colours of an English winter sky. Even so I suppose they must have a particular name, but as geology, like astronomy, is one of those subjects I wish I knew something about, but don't, I really have no idea what it might be. They look to be slate, but if they were, you'd expect some of them to have knife-sharp edges where they have split, but for the most part these are all smooth and round and feel so comfortable in the hand, but sometimes when you pick one up you find there are round holes in it. Unbelievably, I have learned, they are formed by molluscs called *piddocks* that are capable of boring their way inside! And of course there are stones which have been worn down into disks and are just perfect for playing ducks and drakes. Among the drab grey, and all the brighter for the contrast, there are the speckled granites and quartz, and, by no means unattractive, there are house bricks that have had all their edges rolled away and softened by the waves and lie about looking like pale red handbags.

I always hope when I am wandering along that I am going to find something *rich and strange,* as Ariel sang in *The Tempest,* but I never have. What does astonish me though is the number of shoes you find. Rubber gloves I can understand. Deckhands might drop them or throw them away when they start to wear out. But shoes? And so many oranges. And of course yards and yards of orange plastic twine. That seems to be quite indestructible. As does all the other plastic, like bottles of Toilet

Cleanser — they can't have got there by accident.

But some things do *suffer a sea-change*. Especially bits of broken glass. Glass started off as sand and the sea seems determined to have it back again, but small fragments can often be seen glittering among the pebbles. One of my favourite American poets, Amy Clampitt, wrote a poem about her collection of them. She could identify, being American, the "amber of Budweiser", but there was also the lapis of Phillips' Milk of Magnesia, and some blurred amethyst "of no known origin".

There are plenty of natural things to be found. At high water mark there are those endless tangles of seaweed that tend to stink most foully in hot weather and be full of flies and sand-hoppers, but there are always shells to be found too. Shells that are almost always empty. Cockles of course, and all sorts and colours of periwinkles, razor shells and the tiny tellins, and those spirals, like white corkscrews, that were once whelks. The ghosts of crabs, starfish so dry they break when you try to pick them up, and jellyfish that themselves slowly dry out until they are just a faint stain on the sand. Cuttlefish, that budgies like so much, fragile sea urchins and those flat, black and somewhat sinister things we call *Mermaids Purses*, but which are the egg cases of dogfish and sometimes there are bits of *sponge* that aren't sponge either but the egg cases of the whelk.

I find it very nearly impossible to walk along a beach without picking up something to take home with me, and I have window sills covered in *treasures.* I also have a collection of birds' skulls on top of a chest of drawers in my study, some of the most prized being an oyster-catcher, a gannet and a curlew. Looking at the length — a full five inches — of the curlew's bill, I can never understand how it manages to open it when it is buried down in the wet sand. The oystercatcher I found had been ringed and the BTO astonished me by telling me that it had been born on Walney and was twenty-seven years old. I would never have guessed they lived so long. It is the gannet that is the most impressive. The beak is massive and a blackbird's skull would fit easily into its eyehole! It took some cutting off too. Diving into the sea from the height it does, it needs powerful neck muscles and it took a pair of secateurs and a scalpel to get through them. Not everyone appreciates this collection, but skulls have a strange beauty to them I find.

One discovery I made on a beach was very unnerving. It was a bottle. I saw it sticking up out of the sand and as I got closer to it I could see that it had a cork in it and then that there was a piece of rolled-up paper in it. A message in a bottle. How romantic. But on that piece of paper I could see, as I bent down to pick it up, one word and one word only and that was my own name. In bold capital letters: **NEIL**. I froze. It seemed so impossible. I really did not know what to do with it. But when I opened it I found that it wasn't anything supernatural, but a questionnaire from a geography student in the Isle of Man who was conducting a tide survey and we just happened to have the same first name. He shook me though.

I have often thought how good it would be to have a house overlooking the sea. I thought that when I was at Braystones, but if I did I fear I would get nothing done. It does have such a pull. In *The Road to the Gunpowder House* I wrote a poem called *Not Exactly Beachcombing* which ends:

> Always I know I'll pick up something
> and take it home with me. I have to.
> It's not that they're mementoes or even
> talismans. I think it's that the sea
> has always bothered me. It seems so
> like the edge of the beyond, the chaos
> our desire for order hurls itself against.
> Coming and going, there's no coping with such
> violent and controlled discord. I suppose I'm
> always hoping one day it will have left behind
> something to explain itself. It could be that.

Ten:

Haverigg. "Escape to Light". RAF Museum.
Haverigg Prison. The Duddon. Wordsworth's
Sonnets. Wonderful Walker. The Hudddlestons The
Castle. Old Trinity Church. Discovery of iron ore
at Hodbarrow. The sea walls. Closure of mines
and ironworks. Borwick Rails Harbour. Two
lighthouses. The Outer Barrier. Steel Green. Millom
Folk Museum. Norman Nicholson.

Near the Inshore Rescue Station at Haverigg stands the last sculpture completed by Josefina de Vasconcellos. She was 91 at the time and conceded that she had needed some help in the 'roughing out', which is

Above: The old lighthouse, Millom.

174

hardly surprising as the piece, called *Escape to Light,* was carved from a seven tonne block of magnesium limestone. *Escape to Light* is a powerful and moving piece of work. The head of a dragon represents evil and wickedness, but the spirit of man is escaping through its wide-open mouth. And on the other side are reliefs of wind, waves and wild geese combining in the upward flight to freedom. The great thing about sculpture, especially in a position like this, is that you can and need to touch it.

I suppose flight is a appropriate theme at this point on the coast as just outside Haverigg there is the *RAF Millom Museum.* RAF Millom itself opened in 1941 as a bombing and gunnery school, with sixteen hundred airmen and airwomen stationed there at its height — quite a culture shock for them and for Millom too I would have thought. But when the war ended it ceased to be operational and was shut down in 1946. In 1953 it did re-open as an Officer Cadet Training Unit, but closed once again after only twelve months and after that various army regiments passed through it sporadically during the early sixties, but it never again had a fixed purpose until the prison service took it over in 1967.

Strange to say, a decisive moment was to take place in September 1992 when the then governor, Bernard Wilson, decided to celebrate the prison's 25th anniversary with a weekend display of its RAF history, and something about that weekend must have caught the imagination, as a group of prison staff and ex-service personnel decided among themselves that it really could not be allowed simply to fizzle out and be a forgotten part of history again. The unbelievable amount of effort they put in has resulted in a slightly chaotic and consequently a rather exciting museum, housed in what was once the Officers' Mess. It has been owned and run since 2000 by Glynn Griffith who, as he admits, never was in the RAF himself. He was in the Police, a community bobby in Millom for thirty years and is still not sure how he ever got involved in it, but involved he is. What's more, he now has a rank and a uniform, as he runs the local ATC.

Outside the Museum stands a bright yellow Westland Whirlwind Helicopter of the RAF Rescue Unit. When you see that, you know you haven't lost your way and then once you are inside its warren of buildings you find yourself among a truly astonishing display of items they have amassed over the years. The first thing you see is not actually an RAF plane at all, but an HM14 *Pou de Ciel* or "Flying Flea", a tiny little plane which was assembled out of a kit manufactured in France. An Ulverston eccentric bought it, put it together, towed it to the beach and took off in it, but not actually knowing how to fly. Not surprisingly, it did a nose-dive and crashed into the sand. He was lucky though and got away with his life, while the plane was carted away and put back together for the museum by what Glynn described as "the acclaimed aircraft restoration workshop in Haverigg prison."

The other items you see as you work your way through the five separate buildings are of course far more serious and some are rather grim. There are machine guns and what is left of the cockpit of a Spitfire in which some young man must have died. It looks so small and cramped. And alongside it is a large coloured photograph to show what it was like when it was being flown. What it makes you realise is that with all its dials and equipment in place it was even more cramped.

The Museum houses both the massive and the tiny: hundreds of model aeroplanes alongside the Rolls Royce engines which flew the actual planes themselves. One display is of an aircraft mechanic's toolkit and it seems shockingly primitive: hacksaws and massive hammers, files and screwdrivers and various sorts and sizes of pliers. And yet this is what kept Bomber Command in the air.

The technology on board the planes looks no more sophisticated. The wireless operators sat in front of enormous boxes with dials the size of their own faces and knobs so big it must at times have taken both hands to turn them.

As well as the machinery, there is also the human element: a collection of more than five thousand photographs. Young men and girls smiling at you. The girls sporting some remarkable hairdo's. They look so young. It is very moving, but pinned up on the wall and most moving of all are those telegrams which families everywhere must have dreaded receiving. They are so blunt as to be almost brutal . "Regret to inform you your son …… missing in operational flight. Letter follows." So lacking in feeling. It does not only feature the RAF. The other forces are represented here too. There are the uniforms of each of the Guards Regiments as well as the air raid wardens, the land girls and the nurses.

There is a re-creation of an ARP (Air Raid Precaution) Post and even an Anderson Shelter.

The opposition is not forgotten here either. There is a whole room of German memorabilia: a flag with its black swastika emblem in the centre, rows of medals, some look to be Iron Crosses, and there are complete uniforms, including that of an SS officer. It is so very black and so very, very sinister, those jackboots and that swept-up hat with its silver skull. It is not something you can look at for long.

There are records of what the civilians suffered too: photographs of the bomb damage in Liverpool. St James's Station is no more than a column of bricks. St Luke's Church and St Michael's Church both destroyed. Lewis's Department store burned out and a terrible picture of the rubble which a few hours earlier had been Scotland Road. Then there are display cases with fascinatingly random items from the time: ration books, tins of Dried Milk, and a little tin of *Pink Ointment* whatever that might have been.

The helicopter that stands outside the museum reminds us of the RAF Mountain Rescue team as this is where it began. Born out of necessity in 1941 when planes, flown by recruits, started to go down among the Lake District Fells, it was finally recognised as a purpose-trained unit in 1944 and now, as locals know, will also go to the rescue of tourists who get themselves into trouble.

There is so much in this museum. Over 3000 visitors come to it every year and it is growing bigger by the day, as service personnel who fought in the war die and their relatives find suitcases of things they had kept to remember it all. They bring them to the Millom RAF Museum and nothing is ever thrown away. Storage is the problem and plans are in hand to open further sites in Millom and one in Bootle. But, as Glynn Griffith told me, it will never have official recognition as a museum. The officials who came to inspect it could not believe what they saw. *Quirky*, he thinks, was the word one of them used. Flatterer! In museums, all the items have to be in locked display cases or in securely roped-off areas, but in Millom people were being allowed to wander about at their leisure and, horror of horrors, they were even allowed to *handle* the items! You can't be doing that.

In 1967, when the last of the service personnel had finally moved out, what had been RAF Millom became Haverigg Prison. I heard someone pontificating on the radio recently that prisoners went into jail uneducated and unskilled and came out again unskilled and uneducated, and while I accept that in some cases there is probably an element of truth in this, it is not something that can be said of Haverigg's five hundred and sixty-five prisoners. Admittedly, when I was taken on a tour of the prison, it was brief and possibly selective, but I think I saw enough to come out with the feeling that a lot was being done for the prisoners there and that it was a caring institution. In one building prisoners were being taught interior decorating and were given small rooms to practice in. It was serious work that was going on there and the skill of one of the young men hanging wallpaper was far beyond anything I have ever managed. I couldn't feel the joins, let alone see them. Very often, when Haverigg is mentioned locally, you hear people say, "They make garden furniture there, don't they?" And they do. And chairs and tables and sheds, even conservatories. Much of it being made to order. The quality of the work is such that the prison recently won the contract to build three bird-hides for the South Walney Nature Reserve and they would have had to be well-built to withstand the use and battering from the weather they will get there.

What struck me was not just the quiet hard work that was going on, but the relaxed and friendly atmosphere that there was between prisoners and staff. It stemmed, I think, from a mutual respect. Of course it has not always been sweetness and light. In 1999 there was a riot and over 100 prisoners smashed windows and started fires and did over a million pounds worth of damage, but perhaps lessons were learned then. Kenny Evans, the Community and Voluntary Sector Manager who took me round the prison, showed me the different types of cell. The basic is very basic and reminded me of Slade Prison and the kind of thing that housed Norman Stanley Fletcher in *Porridge*. In the next level the individual cells are not kept locked and so there is more freedom of movement and the very best do have a degree of comfort, but that comfort has to be earned and once earned I doubt if any inmate wants to loose it. A sensible system, it seems to me.

As well as the practical training that goes on, the prison library runs a five-week course for Dads in conjunction with Cumbria Library Services. On one afternoon a week, a librarian brings in a *story-sack*. It is a sack which contains a children's book together with a selection of items that might relate to it. For instance, Martin Waddell's *Owl Babies* might have some fluffy toy owls and facts about real owls and perhaps the Muncaster Owl Centre. The dads practice their reading skills and are shown how to make reading to their children a two-way experience. At the end of the course they choose a book to read to their own child and a CD is made of their reading and sent to them. Those who have worked in the IT Centre can even add sound effects — the hooting of owls, wind in the trees and so on. Learning of this made my brief look inside the visiting area all the more poignant. There was a bright crèche area, staffed by kindly volunteers, for the tiny ones, but what most caught my eyes was the smile on the face of the prisoner who was holding his young daughter on his knee. There is so much about Haverigg that is positive and it may only be a Category C Prison and can afford to be more relaxed, but, even so, there is still a four metre high fence around it, topped off by rolls of razor wire. It is not exactly a homely place, but at least when the prisoners do get home they will have been shown the value of staying there.

Having started at the Solway Firth, we are at last, at Haverigg, within sight of the Duddon Estuary where the border of the old county of Cumberland once ran. The River Duddon was always a favourite with Wordsworth, second only to the Derwent, and the sequence of sonnets he wrote about it in 1820 were among the first of his poems to be widely accepted and admired. And it is not difficult to see why. They were not shockingly new and political like some of his earlier pieces on beggars and idiots and they were far easier to understand than his more philosophical works such as the *Immortality Ode.* These were more in the tradition of eighteenth century landscape poems; readers knew where they were with them.

Wordsworth had known the Duddon since his school days. He tells us that as a child he had been taken fishing up near its source by a Hawkshead man. "We fished a great part of the day with very sorry success, the rain pouring torrents, and long before we got home I was worn out with fatigue; and if the good man had not carried me upon his back, I must have lain down under the best shelter I could find. Little did

I then think it would have been my lot to celebrate, in a strain of love and admiration, the stream which for many years I never thought of without recollections of disappointment and distress."

But over the years it began to have even happier associations for him. He went on a walking tour with his wife, Mary, in 1811, and later wrote, "I have many affecting remembrances of Duddon, especially things that occurred on its banks during the later part of that visit." Put like that it sounds quite cheeky, but maybe I am misreading it.

In the *Sonnets* he traces the river from its source in the 'lofty wastes' to where it begins to quicken in a 'garb of snow-white foam' and down to Wrynose Bottom where the first wild flowers are to be seen and 'birch trees risen in silver colonnade'. Then on it goes, 'a brook of loud and stately march', over waterfalls through fields and out to the sea. But the sequence isn't all landscape. There is also, as we would expect, a strong emotional response to each place the river passes through, a sense of its history, and an awareness of the people who have lived there, from stone-age hunters and Roman soldiers to near contemporaries. There is a fine poem on Seathwaite Chapel which celebrates the Reverend Robert Walker, a man of the humblest of origins, who had been its curate from 1735 to 1802. He was ninety-three when he died there and he became known as *Wonderful Walker*, not because he was a wonderful walker, as is sometimes thought (especially by Lake District walkers) but because he was a wonderful man — compassionate, virtuous and industrious. Wordsworth added a six thousand word *note* to the sonnet sequence extolling him and ending by saying one might have thought that "one of the apostles had returned to mortality, and in that vale of peace had come to exemplify the beauty of holiness in the life and character of Mr Walker."

The Millom poet, Norman Nicholson, took issue with Wordsworth in his poem *To The River Duddon*. Wordsworth had described it as "remote from every taint of sordid industry", but writing in 1944, when the ironworks dominated the skyline, this amused Nicholson and he described the slag banks, the sinter dust, and all the gullies stained with ore. But by the time of his last collection, *Sea To The West,* in 1981 all was changed again and in his poem *The Dismantling of Millom Ironworks* he admitted that he'd "laughed once at those words" but now he not only took them back, he was wondering about what future changes might be.

> And maybe the ghost of Wordsworth, seeing further than I can,
> Will stare from Duddon Bridge, along miles of sand and
> mudflats
> To a peninsular bare as it used to be, and, beyond, to a river
> Flowing, untainted now, to a bleak, depopulated shore.

There is little to be gained from arguing the merits of various Lake District *views*. They are countless and each one is somebody's favourite, but all the same, I would contend that the view of the Duddon estuary you get from the top of the hill above Grizebeck does take some beating. So much smaller than the Solway Firth or Morecambe Bay, it is a prospect the eye can take in completely, enclosed as it is by the rounded backdrop of Black Combe, at the foot of which, Millom, with its church spire so dominant, can look positively picturesque when the sun is shining on it.

But for more than a hundred years, from the middle of the nineteenth century right up until the 1970's, when it was home to the Millom Iron Works, it was anything but picturesque. The aerial photographs of what it was like in the 1960's show us something which, even though it does have a certain grandeur, is still unbelievably ugly. The foundry itself was well over two hundred yards long and seventy feet high. Yet now there is not a single trace of it anywhere, which is perhaps a pity. Writing in his book *Cumberland Iron,* in 1969, the year after the works were closed down, A. Harris described "the gaunt remains of engine houses and chimneys, the ruins of workshops and stores and the tracks of numerous mineral railways combining to create a landscape which is unique in South Lakeland." He suggests that it would be a fascinating place for the industrial archaeologist, which it might well have been, but they were not given the chance and there is nothing whatsoever there now. It was all quickly shovelled away as if it were something to be ashamed of, yet the mines and the Iron Works *were* Millom and the town itself can hardly be said to have existed before them. The census returns for 1841 show only 356 people living there and twenty years later there were still under one thousand, but then iron ore was discovered and by the end of the century the population had swollen to over ten thousand. A rural economy, probably a subsistence economy, had become an area of heavy industry in a few decades. More than a thousand men were working underground at one time and very few of them would have been born in the area; they were Cornish, Welsh and Irish.

Yet in one respect Millom can be said to have hardly changed in all those years, as what is known as Millom today had always been known as Holborn Hill – nothing to do with the London Holborn, but a farmstead named, in all probability after a Viking settler by the name of Hallbjörn. Millom was at least a mile north of that and consisted of a castle, a church and a few farms. And they are still there.

Millom is probably the only Cumberland Manor recorded in the Domesday Book, having been included as part of Amounderness, under York and the castle can be traced back to a motte built on the present site in the early years of the twelfth century to defend the ford-crossing into Furness. It was held by the Boisvilles family for over a hundred years until the male line ran out and Joan de Boisvilles married Sir John Huddleston, whose family then held it for the next five hundred years. The Hudddlestons were evidently a prosperous and successful family from the very start.. The castle was fortified and embattled by royal license in 1355 and by the seventeenth century had become elegant enough to be recorded as having a well-stocked deer park, and a print dated 1739 shows it to have been a truly imposing structure.

They were also a powerful family, enjoying "jure regalia", that is complete jurisdiction over their entire seignority, a jurisdiction which was totally independent of the sheriff, and one which literally gave them the power of life and death. They must have used that power too, as they had a gallows erected on a nearby hill and a recent plaque records that "Here the Lords of Millom exercised Jure Regalia". A powerful family and of course a military family, doing battle at Bannockburn, Agincourt and Bosworth Field. And devoted royalists. Sir William Huddleston, one of nine brothers who fought on the King's side in the Civil War, raised a regiment of foot which was defeated at Lindal-in-Funress. He was taken prisoner and unfortunately the castle was besieged by Parliamentary troops and partially destroyed in 1644.

There is an interesting, and very royalist, family story that one John Huddleston, a Catholic priest ordained at Douai, helped Charles II to escape after the defeat at Worcester and so gained royal protection after

Millom Castle

the Restoration. The story goes on to say that as Charles was dying, his brother, the Duke of York, brought the priest to the King's bedside saying, "Sire, this good man once saved your life. He now comes to save your soul." Huddleston heard his confession and Charles died a Catholic.

The castle was repaired after the damage of the Civil War but by 1739 was in ruins again and in 1774 the estate was sold for little more than £20,000 to Sir James Lowther. Nothing of the castle can be seen from the road today, but the ruins are still there and far more extensive than you would ever expect. What really fascinates me about though it that there is still a family living in the Pele Tower and that that same family is running a thriving and state-of-the-art dairy farm.

Alongside the castle, and probably once enclosed within its moat, is Old Trinity Church, which dates back as early as 1160, but which has undergone three major bouts of such extensive 'restoration' so that the uninitiated can no longer tell what's what, but it is good to see that its first vicar was simply called Adam. As you'd expect, there is a Huddleston Family Chapel with the sandstone tomb of Sir John Huddleston, the Yorkist who fought for Richard III at Bosworth Field, and a fine alabaster monument commemorating his grandson, Richard, who is shown in full armour and with his wife Elizabeth Dacre lying beside him.

Another footnote from Huddleston family history shows the direction that the area was soon to take, when Ferdinand Huddleston had the oak trees in the park cut down to supply fuel for his iron smelting furnace, and this was in 1690. Mining on a small scale was being carried out even in Roman times, but it was not until the middle years of the nineteenth century that it became an industry when Lord Lonsdale granted a licence to search for minerals in the area around Hodbarrow. It was hard work, drilling down through the rock, sinking shafts and cutting out underground levels and it was expensive too. Nathaniel Caine, one of the original shareholders in the enterprise, records that they had spent £57,000 before they made their first profit. But their perseverance paid off when they hit on a vein one hundred feet think and of quite exceptional quality. Soon there were cargoes of iron ore being shipped to South Wales, the Mersey and the Dee from the burgeoning harbour at Borwick Rails. By 1866 the weekly output was 3,000 tons and there were 300 men working underground.

This growth in population meant that houses had to be built, and schools and shops, chapels and hospitals. Millom was beginning to take shape as a town, but the living conditions were such that in Company houses where shift workers lived it was said that the beds never got cold. One of these *housing projects* rejoiced in the unsentimental name of Concrete Square and was still in use until 1973 when it was finally demolished.

While the success brought a certain degree of prosperity, it also brought with it a new problem: the vein was running out under the sea and it was not long before subsidence began to occur below high water line. If there had been a collapse then the entire workings would have been flooded by seawater. Work on a sea wall began in 1888 and took two years to complete, but after only eight years there was further subsidence and part of it fell. The value of the ore that was there under the sea can be seen from the cost of the wall built to replace it: £60,000 and that was in

1905. It still stands today, but instead of holding back the sea, the area behind it has been allowed to flood so that it now encloses a marina and nature reserve.

In the 113 years that the Hodbarrow Mines were in operation twenty-five million tons of iron ore were extracted. Sometimes it was as much as half a million tons in a year, but by 1967 it was under thirty thousand. Closure, it was announced, would be in March 1968, but the managing Director was at pains to stress that this would have no effect on the Millom Iron Works with which it had been amalgamated since 1958. This of course was not true. It too had a history going back a hundred years, but in June of that same year it too ceased production. In September 400 men walked from the Iron Works gates to Millom town centre carrying a mock coffin and a banner spelling out the town's name:

Misled, **I**gnored, **L**ost, **L**ied to, **O**verlooked **M**en. But it was all a lost cause. The government could have bought the entire operation for £1, but they decided against it. Like Czechoslovakia a few decades before, Millom was a far-away place of which they knew little, and cared even less. The Labour MP for Barrow blamed it all on the failure of private enterprise and argued that the government could not be expected to plough money into a firm that wasn't commercially viable. Men went on the dole and Norman Nicholson describes them:

> … morning after morning, there
> They stand, by the churchyard gate,
> Hands in pockets, shoulders to the slag,
> The men whose fathers stood there back in '28
> When their sons were at school with me.
> The town
> Rolls round the century's black orbit.

The official line was that they were skilled men who would soon find work elsewhere. but as one man told the local paper, 'No one wants to buy a house in Millom, so we're stuck.'

The best way to get an impression of what Millom was and what it is like now is to set off from the Square along Devonshire Road — noticing as you do another of Colin Telfer's works: an iron ore miner jamming a metal bar between the spokes of an ore-tub to bring it to a stop. That was the only braking system they had; health & safety please note. Then on past the library, a fine sandstone building, and you can tell how old it is by the words set into its façade: *PUBLIC READING ROOM* and *FREE LIBRARY* . Beyond that, and in between the sedate new houses, you can catch occasional glimpses of the slag banks — grassed over now and covered in gorse and looking like a natural feature of the landscape. One of the things I noticed along Devonshire Road was the constant *cheep cheep* of house sparrows. They have become almost rare in some parts — certainly where I live — but not in Millom. At the end of the road is the Duddon Pilot Inn, which as well as serving good lunches has a wonderful collection of old photographs on its walls as well as other bits and pieces. There was once another Inn just called The Pilot. It was on Holborn Hill and was famous among other things for the sign which read: "William and Ann Barren live heare, who mostly keep good ale and beer, 1745. You that intend to cross ye sand, call here a gide at your command."

At the end of Devonshire Road is a track that goes through where the ironworks once were and leading to Borwick Rails Harbour. It comes as complete surprise if you don't know the area. There is a slight rise in the path and when you get to the top there is the whole of the Duddon Estuary suddenly before you and the hills of Low Furness so unexpectedly close. And as you turn and look to your left, there are the main hills of the Lake District and of course Black Combe wearing as ever a cloud for a hat. Borwick Rails Harbour is now no more than a row of ragged and rotting wooden piles and massive iron bolts which were once the jetty, but it stretches for a hundred yards or so and you do get an impression of what it must have been like when thousands of tons of ore were being shipped out of there every week.

The soft sand doesn't make for easy walking.. It is always hard to know which is worse — pebbles that shift under your feet and can cripple you or sand that you sink into. But this is a very beautiful beach. There are redshanks calling and skylarks and it is remarkably litter-free. At the right time of year there is also the rich molasses smell of silage. After a short while there is a track that leads off the beach and up to an old windmill. When it ceased work as a mill, it served as the first offices of the iron ore mining company and the very first mine, Towsey Hole, was nearby. Down on the shore the rocks still have clear traces of iron in them. There is a splendid view of Hodbarrow Harbour from there and of the old

The Old Windmill, Millom

stone lighthouse, which was built in 1866 and is still standing solid as the rocks around it with not a stone out of place. Ironically, it easily outlasted the new iron one which was built to replace it in 1905, but which by 1949, when trade at Duddon Port had declined and output in the mine fallen drastically, was closed down. The light went out, the years passed and it slowly became an unsightly rusting wreck, but the Children of Haverigg school had adopted it as their logo in 1997 and they it was who first campaigned to have it restored. £20,000 of Heritage Lottery money was raised and in 2004 it was re-opened. And with a wonderful sense of history the opening ceremony was performed by Jacqueline Barrett, whose father-in-law had performed the same ceremony all those years before. Freshly painted, it looks splendid again now; it is solar-powered, and the children of Haverigg School have been appointed, and quite right too, as honorary lighthouse keepers.

On a wall behind the lighthouse there is a plaque giving details of the history of the light and of the mines. My favourite piece records that in

1854 the *Ulverston Advertiser* advertised the sale of Hodbarrow Farm, but failed to mention the possibility of there being iron ore beneath it. Instead they suggested that it might make a most lucrative investment if it were to be converted into a public bathing resort! It was in the very next year that the Earl of Lonsdale granted a license to search for minerals and John Barrett sank the first shaft at Towsey Hole. There would be no public bathing there.

What you are walking along here is the Outer Barrier which was built in 1905 and was a major piece of civil engineering. Constructed of two parallel banks of limestone, it is more than a mile and a quarter long, forty feet high and over eighty feet wide at the top and was built to safeguard an area of 170 acres where the most active mining was being carried out. Near the half-way point, as you look inland, you can see the remains of the old inner barrier, built as a rigid wall, which had taken two years to construct but then collapsed after no more than eight.

At the end of the barrier you come to the village of Steel Green, but you can hardly call it a village now; it is a huge caravan camp, nearly all the houses that used to be there having been demolished in 1983. The few which do remain suggest it had had some elegance to it once, and round behind the caravans you come to what is a very imposing building, now the Commodore Hotel, but which in its time has been Millom's Fever Hospital and the Head Office of Hodbarrow Mines.

Back again in Millom, if you want to know more, then there is The Folk Museum, attached to the railway station where there is a very realistic mock-up of an iron ore pit shaft. All the bits and pieces are authentic and it is convincingly dirty too. The most alarming feature to my mind though is that the miner, in his raggedy-torn clothes, is not wearing anything like a hard hat. He is sporting a felt one, with a candle somehow fastened to the front! It is a wonder any of them survived.

The museum also features the other inhabitants of Millom. There is a blacksmiths, a wheelwright's shop and the agricultural side is not forgotten either. Then there is a display of women's clothes, with some astonishing underwear, and they have re-created a whole street with what were called "Front-room shops" where housewives sold a few basic items such as cocoa, cigarettes and matches and a washing powder called *Rinso*. At the end of the street is the interior of an *everyday home,* but it looks rather middle class to me, as it has a gramophone and a stuffed bird on the dresser. But the homemade toys, the rag mat on the floor and the stone hot water bottle probably bring back memories to some of its visitors, and the mangle must, surely, manufactured by C. Pennington & Sons of Ulverston.

One of the Museum's fullest displays is devoted to the poet, Norman Nicholson, who was born in St George's Terrace, Millom, in 1914, in what was then his father's *Gentleman's Outfitters.* He lived there all his life until he died in 1987. Among all the photographs of him and other memorabilia I am always intrigued to look at the pages of his own totally illegible handwriting, mercifully alongside printed translations. And now there is a plaque above the door in St George's Terrace which reads "Home of Cumbrian Poet NORMAN NICHOLSON Man of Millom. 1914-1987" and both those titles are right. He was a Cumbrian poet and more so, in many ways, than the Romantics, those we know as the *Lake District Poets.* When you look down the index of his first collection, *Five Rivers,* published in 1944, you don't see the famous Lake District names such as Hawkshead and Grasmere; instead there are Egremont, Cleator Moor, Whitehaven and Askam, which, for all their merits, could never be said to be romantic. It was this which earned him the rather dismissive label of *Provincial Poet*, a label which was still sticking to him when The Times printed his obituary. But Nicholson asserted the importance of writing about the area and the town he knew, defiantly giving his 1972 collection the title *A Local Habitation.* It is in this that we meet with such poems as *On the Closing of Millom Ironworks.*

In 1977 he received the Queen's Medal for Poetry and in 1981 he was awarded the O.B.E. His reputation is firmly established now. There is a Norman Nicholson Society and a Memorial Window to him in St George's Church. Designed by Christine Boyce, the window, as she has explained, does not seek to illustrate Nicholson's verse, but to evoke it. It took her nearly two years even to complete the design and the finished work is an intricate blend of brief quotations from some of the poems together with shapes and colours inspired by them. It is a window not simply to be glanced at in passing but one which repays — and with binoculars, as she suggests — some quiet moments of study. Christine Boyce has written a pamphlet about the window and how she made it and this is on sale in the church.

I myself was both delighted and honoured to be asked to edit Norman Nicholson's *Collected Poems* which were published in 1994 and in that year I gave several talks and reading around the country — none more memorable of course than the one I gave in Millom. But what I recall most fondly was that when I had finished speaking, Nicholson's literary executor, Irvine Hunt, came forward to say that he had a promise to keep. Norman had said to him once, "If anyone ever edits my collected poems I want you to buy the poor bugger a bottle of whiskey from me." I had from time to time drunk a good malt with Norman. He had a collection of empties which ran right round the top of the kitchen work surface. To receive one from him from beyond the grave was a very moving experience. And I have kept the bottle.

I have one other reason to be grateful to Norman Nicholson. In the topographical books he wrote, *Cumberland and Westmorland, Portrait of the Lakes,* and *Greater Lakeland,* it was the traditional areas, what one might call the Tourist Areas of the lake District he wrote about so tellingly. He did not, fortunately for me, write at any length about the industrial coast. If he had, perhaps I would never have been asked to write this book, and so would never have met the many people who talked to me wherever I went. I would never have visited some of the out-of-the-way places I went to, nor discovered so much that I never knew about the county I live in.

INDEX